AUSTIN
3:16 316 Facts and Stories about

StoneCold
Steve Austin

MICHAEL McAVENNIE

Copyright © WWE, 2021

Published by ECW Press
665 Gerrard Street East
Toronto, ON M4M 1Y2
416-694-3348 / info@ecwpress.com

Editor for the press: Michael Holmes
Cover design and images: WWE
Type design: Troy Cunningham
Interior images: Anthony Ruttgaizer;
ripped paper ©happymeluv

Library and Archives Canada
Cataloguing in Publication

Title: Austin 3:16 : 316 facts and stories
about Stone Cold Steve Austin / Michael
McAvennie.

Other titles: 316 facts and stories about
    Stone Cold Steve Austin | Three
    hundred sixteen facts and stories about
    Stone Cold Steve Austin

Names: McAvennie, Michael, author.
Identifiers: Canadiana (print) 20200393944
    | Canadiana (ebook) 20200394487

    ISBN 978-1-77041-616-1 (softcover)
    ISBN 978-1-77305-723-1 (EPUB)
    ISBN 978-1-77305-724-8 (PDF)
    ISBN 978-1-77305-725-5 (Kindle)

Subjects: LCSH: Austin, Steve, 1964-—
    Miscellanea. | LCSH: Wrestlers—
    United States—Biography—Miscellanea.
    | LCGFT: Trivia and miscellanea.

Classification: LCC GV1196.A97 M33
    2021 | DDC 796.812092—dc23

Printing: Friesens 1 2 3 4 5
Printed and bound in Canada

To my son, Cillian, whose boundless enthusiasm makes "The Lad & Dad Connection" an unbeatable tandem, and our manager Áine, aka "The Mam." The two of you make me feel like a World Champion every day.

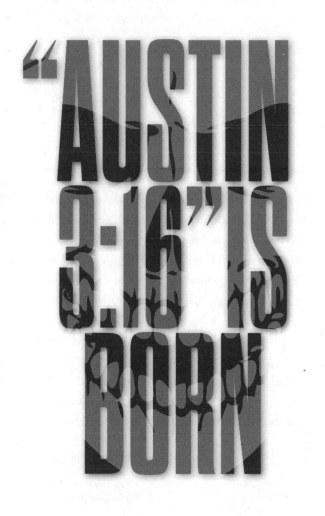

"The first thing I want to be done is to get that piece of crap [Jake Roberts] out of my ring! Don't just get him out of the ring, get him out of [WWE]! Because I've proved, son, without a shadow of a doubt, you ain't got what it takes anymore!

"You sit there, and you thump your Bible and you say your prayers, and it didn't get you anywhere! Talk about your Psalms, talk about John 3:16 . . . Austin 3:16 says, 'I just whipped your ass!'

"All he's got to do is buy him a cheap bottle of Thunderbird and try to dig back some of that courage he had in his prime! As the King of the Ring, I'm servin' notice to every one of the [WWE] Superstars! I don't give a damn what they are, they're *all* on the list, and that's Stone Cold's list, and I'm fixing to start running through all of 'em!

"As far as this championship match is considered, son, I don't give a damn if it's Davey Boy Smith or Shawn Michaels. Steve Austin's time has come, and when I get the shot, you're looking at the next [WWE] Champion! And that's the bottom line, 'cause Stone Cold said so!"

Stone Cold Steve Austin's historic comments to Dok Hendrix (aka Michael P.S. Hayes) and the WWE Universe at the MECCA Arena in Milwaukee, WI (*King of the Ring*, June 23, 1996)

WHO IS STONE COLD STEVE AUSTIN?

Stone Cold Steve Austin was born Steven James Anderson of Austin, TX. His mother, Beverly, was a single parent raising Steve and his brothers, Scott and Kevin, in Victoria, TX, before she met Ken Williams, an insurance salesman who also split his time as a cattle rancher and country singer. After marrying Beverly in 1968, Williams adopted the three boys, gave them his surname, and moved the family to Edna, TX, a small town 100 miles south of Houston with a population that ranged from 5,332 to 5,650. The Williams family eventually added another boy, Jeff, and a girl, Jennifer.

OKAY, HOW DID STEVE WILLIAMS BECOME STEVE *AUSTIN*?

When Steve Williams was sent to compete in Memphis, TN–based Mid-South Wrestling in 1989, the promotion's booker, "Dirty" Dutch Mantell — known to the WWE Universe as The Blu Brothers' and Justin Hawk Bradshaw's manager, Uncle Zebekiah, or in more recent years as Zeb Colter — told the very inexperienced rookie he had 15 minutes to come up with a new

moniker. The reason? Mid-South Wrestling already had an established star in "Dr. Death" Steve Williams.

After 15 minutes, the future Stone Cold hadn't come up with a new name. That's when Mantell told him, "Okay, you're Steve Austin."

Williams was concerned that people might think he was ripping off the main character's name from the TV series *The Six Million Dollar Man*. Mantell insisted it would work because the young Texan's name was Steve and he was born in Austin.

Initially, Stone Cold didn't love the name change, but it worked out pretty well for him. So much, in fact, that he legally changed his name to Steve Austin in late 2007.

0:04

REMEMBER THE DATE

Born December 18, 1964, Stone Cold Steve Austin shares his birthday with several celebrities, athletes, and personalities, including fellow WWE Hall of Famer Trish Stratus and WWE/ECW alum Rob Van Dam; Rolling Stones guitarist Keith Richards; pop musicians Sia, Christina Aguilera, and Billie Eilish; and Academy Award winners like director Steven Spielberg and actor Brad Pitt.

0:05

"I want everybody out there in TV Land to touch your
screens and feel what it's like to be destined for success.
Feel what it's like to be born a champion, man!

"I didn't come out here just to run my mouth, Brother Love.
I'm here to prove every single thing I say. Me and The Million
Dollar Man talked. I'm in the Royal Rumble, man. I'm gonna
prove how good The Ringmaster is. After I toss every single
one of the [WWE] Superstars over that rope right there, man,
I'll be the one gettin' the shot at the [WWE] Championship.
It doesn't mean anything compared to the Million Dollar
belt, of course. But in *WrestleMania*, man, I'm gonna do
it all, and you're gonna see what The Million Dollar Man
and the Million Dollar Champ are gonna accomplish!"

Introduced by Ted DiBiase as his Million
Dollar Champion, Steve Austin makes his WWE
debut as "The Ringmaster" on "The Brother
Love Show" (*Raw*, January 8, 1996)

STONE COLD TO A TEA

After multiple failed attempts to find a suitable ring name for his new, edgy, cold-blooded persona, Steve Austin vented his frustrations to then-wife Jeanie Clarke while she made him some tea in their kitchen. Clarke, a Brentwood, England, native who drank tea all the time, tried reassuring Austin, telling him, "Don't worry about it. Just go ahead and drink your tea before it gets stone cold."

Clarke and Austin instantly realized they had the perfect ring name. After running it past WWE for executive approval and legal clearance, Stone Cold Steve Austin was born.

A ROYAL RUMBLER SECOND TO NONE

To this day, Steve Austin is the only WWE Superstar to win the Royal Rumble Match three times. Stone Cold was the last remaining entrant in the 30-man, over-the-top-rope contest in 1997, 1998, and 2001. In 1999, he nearly won his third consecutive Rumble Match.

The magnitude of Austin's accomplishment is significant when you consider the fact that only six Superstars have won two Royal Rumble Matches: Hulk Hogan (1990–91), Shawn Michaels (1995–96), Triple H (2002, 2016), Batista (2005, 2014), John Cena (2008, 2013), and Randy Orton (2009, 2017).

TAKING STUDY BREAKS AT WCCW

S teve Williams grew up a fan of sports entertainment, but his fascination with the industry magnified after transferring from Wharton County Junior College to the University of North Texas in Denton. Since it was only a 35-mile drive to Dallas, he and his college buddies would drive to the famed Dallas Sportatorium, home of World Class Championship Wrestling (WCCW). There, they'd watch the ring action Friday nights and Saturday mornings, the latter being the day for WCCW TV tapings.

It was also during his days at UNT that Williams became more familiar with other televised promotions, including *Power Pro Wrestling* and *Mid-South Wrestling*, which featured an announcer with whom Stone Cold would later develop a lifelong friendship — Jim Ross.

A MIDDLE FINGER TO THE WIND

T hough the age of Austin 3:16 was really picking up steam in 1997, WWE Chairman Vince McMahon once asked if Stone Cold could do a different gesture instead of flipping people off with his middle fingers, to alleviate complaints made by WWE business partners.

"I said, 'No, there's not,'" Austin recollected at a media junket in 2016. "I told Vince I was not going to change sh*t."

The Texas Rattlesnake explained that years of struggling to make a mark in sports entertainment, plus being unceremoniously dismissed by WCW management, had made him frustrated and angry. "I'd be damned if anybody was going to take anything from me," he said. "I'm going to run over you and we're going to the top. Or *I'm* going to the top, and *you're* going to come along for the ride."

Everyone went along for the ride, and Austin pointed the way, using a middle finger.

0:10

EVEN A RATTLESNAKE CAN HAVE FRIENDS

Steve Austin often preferred to work alone when kickin' ass, but he actually paired with 75 tag team partners. Of those 75 partners, 39 were in WWE, where Stone Cold won four World Tag Team Titles. His four co-champions were also multi-time WWE Champions throughout their careers: Shawn Michaels, Dude Love (who won the WWE Title as Mankind), Undertaker, and Triple H.

MORE THAN YOUR AVERAGE JOCK

From his sophomore year in Edna High School, Steve Williams was a varsity starter and All-District running back for the Edna Cowboys. He also threw discus for the school's track and field squad and was an all-star catcher for the baseball team. He even took up tennis for a year — and made it to the state finals — because he wanted to impress a girl.

It should be noted, however, that the man who'd become The Toughest S.O.B. in WWE was also quite the scholar. In fact, his good grades earned him a place among the National Honor Society. *Noblesse oblige*.

"AND THAT'S THE BOTTOM LINE . . . BECAUSE FANG FROST SAID SO"?

Before Steve Austin left his Ringmaster character behind and became Stone Cold, WWE's Creative Services department submitted a list of names for the cold-blooded persona he hoped to evoke. One look at the list, and you'll understand why the department's suggestions . . . well, they left Austin cold.

- Lee Van Slade
- Ice Fury

- Cool Luke
- Luke Randsom
- Morgan Shiver
- Willard Wolfe
- Bitter Payne
- Bitter Von Ruthless
- Fang Frost

- Soldier Steel
- Stiletto
- Captain Bludd
- Scorpion
- Kool-Z
- Krool-T
- Stealth

The list, which circulated to a select few as an interoffice memo, also included a name that Austin had suggested:

- Slade Stone (The Stone Man)

0:13

DRIVING THE ROCK CRAZY

Virginia's Roanoke Civic Center hosted an unforgettable *Raw* moment on December 1, 1997, when Stone Cold Steve Austin drove his Ford F-150 pickup truck into the arena and interrupted a match between Vader and The Nation of Domination's Rocky Maivia.

Though Maivia — or "The Rock," as he began calling himself — eventually won the match, he was clearly driven to distraction while the Intercontinental Champion watched from afar and hoisted some Steveweisers on top of his tricked-out, Stone Cold–themed vehicle. He even cranked up the music on his speakers for the benefit of the arena's capacity crowd.

That night in the "Magic City" represents the first of seemingly countless instances in which The Texas Rattlesnake would commit vehicular mayhem to grind the gears of his adversaries. It was also the first time the WWE Universe saw Austin crack open a beer before, during, or after he cracked some skulls.

A "STUNNING" REPERTOIRE

In his World Championship Wrestling (WCW) days, "Stunning" Steve Austin was regarded as one of the ring's top technical performers. He didn't have the Stone Cold Stunner as his go-to finisher, but he did have the Stun Gun, in which he'd incapacitate opponents by lifting them up thigh-high, then dropping them face-down onto the top ring rope.

In late 1993, even though he had cut ties with his Hollywood Blonds partner, "Flyin'" Brian Pillman, Austin added two Tinseltown-labeled submission maneuvers to his offensive arsenal. If he didn't make you tap out to the Hollywood & Vine (a standing figure-four leglock), he'd roll you up with an inside toehold/leglock combination he called "That's a Wrap." The latter move is reminiscent of Corey Graves's Lucky 13 finisher at NXT, though Austin's take more closely resembled the Fuller Leglock — which is fitting since, during that time, Robert Fuller (aka Colonel Robert Parker) was his manager at WCW.

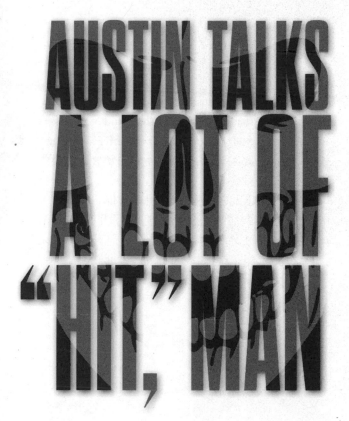

AUSTIN TALKS A LOT OF "HIT," MAN

0:15

"Bret Hart doesn't even qualify as bein' a chicken. He's the slimy substance that runs out of the south end of a chicken. Let me make myself clear: If you put the letter 's' in front of 'Hit Man,' you've had my exact opinion of Bret Hart!"

Stone Cold Steve Austin tells us what he really thinks of The Excellence of Execution at *In Your House: Mind Games*, in Philadelphia, PA's CoreStates Center (September 22, 1996)

PAINE IN THE NECK

The Expendables was a box-office hit in 2010, earning nearly $275 million worldwide and two sequels. For writer, director, and star Sylvester Stallone, the movie is also a painful reminder that one doesn't mess with Stone Cold Steve Austin. While promoting the film, Stallone disclosed in interviews how one fight scene with Austin was so vicious he actually suffered a hairline fracture in his neck and required a metal plate to be surgically inserted.

When *The Expendables* was released on home video, Stallone's audio commentary pointed out a scene when an explosion next to Austin's foot nearly cost The Texas Rattlesnake his leg. Fortunately, Austin, who played rogue mercenary Dan Paine, was holding a bag that acted as a shield when the explosion went off.

HE DRANK *HOW MUCH*?

It's believed that a rattlesnake drinks at least its own body weight in liquid every year. Following that logic, a beer-swigging, 252-pound Texas Rattlesnake would require an annual intake of 3,865.12 fluid ounces.

Stone Cold Steve Austin drank more than a third of his annual amount in *one night*.

Okay, that's a slight exaggeration. He had some help. During a WWE Japan tour in February 2004, the Sheriff of *Raw* issued an in-ring beer bash and celebrated extensively with The Hurricane, The Dudley Boyz, Torrie Wilson, and Stacy Keibler. As he recalled on his podcast, *The Steve Austin Show*, the six Superstars consumed *115 beers* — the most he ever remembers drinking.

Evenly distributing that amount among six people brings the total down to a still-whopping 19 cans of beer per individual (based on a standard beer serving of 12 fluid ounces). And honestly, it's a pretty safe bet that Torrie and Stacy didn't imbibe 38 cans of beer in one night.

Just trying to work out the math on this is enough to give a person a hangover.

0:18

HIGH SCHOOL'S MOST POPULAR COWBOY

I s it really so surprising that arguably the most popular Superstar in sports-entertainment history also grew up well admired by his peers in the hallowed halls of learning? For three consecutive years, Steve Austin — then Steve Williams — was voted Most Popular by his classmates at Edna High School. In his senior year, he earned the distinct title of "Mr. Cowboy," the school equivalent to being homecoming king.

SAY "WHAT?"

With a WWE Championship defense against Kurt Angle loom-ing at *SummerSlam* in August 2001, Stone Cold Steve Austin worked himself back from an injury by getting in ring shape at several WWE live events. While driving to one of those events, a bored Austin left WWE Superstar Christian a long, rambling voicemail in which he'd say something and immediately follow up with a "What?" Being WWE's top villain at the time, he liked the way it sounded and that using it to cut off others from talking was a great way to disrespect them.

Austin's "What?"-laden browbeating achieved the result he wanted with his adversaries. It was a different story with fans attending the venues; rather than jeer Austin, they joined in! Stone Cold soon decided to make asking the question in promos more entertaining than intimidating, and in the process instituted a chanting pastime that decades later continues in arenas everywhere.

"What?"

GREETINGS FROM SPACE CITY, USA

Steve Austin was eight-year-old Steve Williams when he became hooked on sports entertainment. The one sports-entertainment program available to TVs based in Edna, TX, *Houston Wrestling*, run by legendary wrestling promoter Paul Boesch from Space City's Sam Houston Coliseum, became appointment viewing for Williams on the weekends — not necessarily because of the storylines, but because there were rivalries, championships on the line, and lots of punching, kicking, and wrestling in the ring.

0:21

INFLUENCED BY A STONE COLD KILLER

Steve Austin's Stone Cold character was inspired by *The Iceman Tapes: Conversations with a Killer*, a 1992 HBO documentary about convicted serial killer Richard "The Iceman" Kuklinski, whose services were employed by the Genovese, Gambino, and DeCavalcante crime families. Though Austin didn't condone the actions of Kuklinski, who claimed to have murdered more than a hundred people (and stored one corpse in an industrial freezer for two years, thereby earning his nickname), he thought the idea of a cold-blooded man who didn't care about anyone was perfect for his new in-ring attitude.

CHAMPIONSHIP MATERIAL

The Bionic Redneck's ring gear is basic black, but his championship pedigree is very much golden. During his in-ring career, Stone Cold Steve Austin amassed an incredible 19 championships, including:

- six WWE Championships
- four World Tag Team Titles (with Shawn Michaels, Mick Foley/Dude Love, Undertaker, and Triple H)
- two Intercontinental Championships
- one WCW/NWA World Tag Team Championship (with "Flyin'" Brian Pillman)
- two WCW United States Heavyweight Titles
- two WCW World Television Championships
- one TWF (Texas Wrestling Federation) World Tag Team Title (with California Stud)
- one Million Dollar Championship

HE'S FROM *WHERE?*

When "Stunning" Steve Austin made his World Championship Wrestling debut in May 1991, it was announced that he hailed from Hollywood, CA. This was news to Austin, who claimed that he had no idea he was being billed from Tinseltown. It eventually worked to his advantage, however, when he and "Flyin'" Brian Pillman formed The Hollywood Blonds.

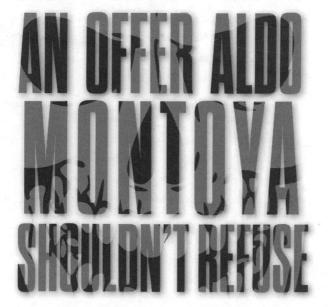

"Here's the story: The whole world knows my name is Stone Cold Steve Austin, and a few people know your name is Aldo Montoya. If I just won the King of the Ring [Tournament], if I just beat the best the [WWE] has to offer, I ain't wrestlin' you. I'm not gonna draw a breath of fresh air and waste it, son. You're a piece of garbage! You don't deserve to be in the same ring with Stone Cold, much less the same state!

"What I'm gonna do is forfeit the match right now, son. I'm gonna forfeit the match out of the goodness of my heart, 'cause I'm in a good mood today. Years from now, you can say to your kids, 'I was fortunate enough to beat Stone Cold in a match. A forfeit no less, but it was a win.'

"The question I'm gonna ask you is: Are you gonna accept the forfeit? Or am I gonna have to go ahead and stomp your little guts in?"

Aldo Montoya takes a verbal beating from Stone Cold before he receives the Stunner [*Superstars of Wrestling*, July 6, 1996]

SCHOLAR AND A "GENTLEMAN"

While watching *World Class Championship Wrestling* on television, Steve Williams started seeing commercials that promoted "Gentlemen" Chris Adams's new wrestling school. After checking out one of the school's seminars and feeling singled out by Adams for his football physique, Williams decided to pay the school's $1,500 enrollment fee and start training.

In addition to mentoring the future Stone Cold Steve Austin, Adams trained other notable sports entertainers, including Awesome Kong, Colt Derringer, Earl Kennedy, Jeanie Clarke, Khris Germany, Tasha Simone, and some outsider by the name of Scott Hall.

BUSY YEAR

Steve Austin was a part of three promotions in 1995. He was Stunning in WCW, an Extreme Superstar in ECW, and because his 1996 debut was pre-recorded at the end of the year, a Ringmaster in WWE. One can even argue Austin's involvement with New Japan Pro-Wrestling as a fourth promotion, though he appeared there as a WCW representative.

AUSTIN'S FIRST MAIN-EVENT *CLASH*

On January 21, 1992, Topeka's Kansas Expocentre hosted WCW's *Clash of the Champions XVIII* and a monster main event: The Dangerous Alliance team of WCW World Television Champion "Stunning" Steve Austin & WCW United States Heavyweight Champion Rick Rude squared off against Ricky "The Dragon" Steamboat & The Man Called Sting. Commentator Jim Ross emphasized the rarity of this match by noting how all four competitors were ranked No. 1 through 4 on the WCW Top 10, meaning they were the four top contenders to the WCW World Heavyweight Title. (Austin was No. 3.)

This marked Austin's first time headlining a *Clash* event, as well as the WCW debut of Jesse "The Body" Ventura. In his always-colorful commentary, Ventura vehemently argued that Austin and Rude didn't lose the match since Sting and Steamboat pinned "Stunning" Steve together.

IN ELITE COMPANY

Only 20 individuals had been recognized as WWE Champion before Stone Cold Steve Austin won sports entertainment's grandest prize in 1998. They are:

- Buddy Rogers
- Bruno Sammartino
- Ivan Koloff
- Pedro Morales
- Stan Stasiak
- Superstar Billy Graham
- Bob Backlund
- The Iron Sheik
- Hulk Hogan
- Andre the Giant

- Randy Savage
- Ultimate Warrior
- Sgt. Slaughter
- Undertaker
- Ric Flair
- Bret Hart
- Yokozuna
- Diesel
- Shawn Michaels
- Sycho Sid

0:29

FIRED BY PHONE AND FEDEX

Steve Austin may not have become the WWE Hall of Famer he is today had he not been fired from World Championship Wrestling (WCW) by Eric Bischoff. Of equal importance is how Bischoff fired him.

On the third night of a three-week WCW tour of Japan in June 1995, Austin tore the right triceps muscle off his elbow. Though he finished the tour, he was incapacitated after returning stateside and had surgery. A few weeks later, Bischoff's assistant asked Austin to call the then-WCW vice president's office. When he did, Bischoff informed him that, based on his salary and on the amount of days he'd been incapacitated, WCW was terminating their agreement with him. A day later, he received the termination notice in writing via Federal Express.

0:30

PILLMAN'S GOT A GUN

More than a week after Stone Cold shattered Brian Pillman's ankle on *Superstars of Wrestling*, The Loose Cannon was laid up in his Walton, KY, home with his family and interviewer Kevin Kelly, wondering if Steve Austin would try keeping his promise of a further beatdown. Austin, of course, did, and Pillman's response — pulling out a 9 mm Glock and pointing it at Stone Cold, plus dropping in an F-bomb on live network TV for good measure — made for an unforgettable and extremely controversial *Raw* moment on November 4, 1996.

The majority of that evening's *Raw* — which moved to its new, earlier timeslot of 8 p.m. EST, in an effort to compete against *WCW Monday Nitro* — had been pre-recorded one week prior. However, the segments with Austin and Pillman that aired via satellite link were shot live, to add realism and tension to the moment. They succeeded all too well. Despite USA Network pre-approving the segment in advance, network executives nearly pulled *Raw* off the air due to the adult, violent nature of Austin's home invasion. Parents and business sponsors like board game giant Milton Bradley also roared at WWE about the non-family friendly programming. WWE would need to tread carefully a while longer before the company's Attitude Era could adapt a TV-14 rating that encouraged parental guidance.

0:31

AUSTIN'S FIRST WWE TITLE DEFENSE

Those attending *Raw* in Philadelphia's CoreStates Center on April 13, 1998, were in for a historic night. Stone Cold Steve Austin was making his first televised WWE Championship defense, and his opponent was none other than WWE's power-drunk Chairman, Vince McMahon. The contest didn't go off as planned, though. First, Mr. McMahon added a stipulation that forced The Texas Rattlesnake to compete with one hand tied behind his back. Then, Dude Love interrupted the bout and attacked Austin with the Mandible Claw.

Though neither champion nor challenger left Philly with a win that night, the Austin-McMahon match delivered a huge victory for WWE. After 83 weeks, *Raw* finally bested *WCW Monday Nitro* in the Nielsen ratings. Such victories would continue to go back and forth until later that year, when WWE firmly dominated the Monday Night War against WCW.

AUSTIN'S *OTHER* FIRST WWE TITLE DEFENSE

Putting up his WWE Championship against Vince McMahon on *Raw* on April 13, 1998, was Stone Cold's first televised title defense. However, he actually had a match nine days earlier that was scheduled to broadcast live from England's "Cottonopolis."

Emanating from the Nynex Arena on April 4, *Mayhem in Manchester* witnessed Steve Austin retain the WWE Title against then-WWE European Champion Triple H, who had just taken over the reins of D-Generation X in place of the injured Shawn Michaels.

Following up on the success of *WWE: One Night Only* in 1997, *Mayhem in Manchester* had been intended as a pay-per-view event that was exclusive to the United Kingdom. However, unexpected roster changes and issues with the venue prompted WWE to cancel its broadcast plans and just release the event later on home video.

Mayhem in Manchester was also the last event to utilize WWE's "New Generation" logo on its promotional materials and ring skirt. A then-new "scratch" logo was more heavily incorporated into the next pay-per-view, *Unforgiven: In Your House* (April 26, 1998).

STONE COLD CONNOISSEUR

During his WWE Hall of Fame career, Stone Cold Steve Austin has consumed countless Steveweisers inside the ring, around the ring, in arena parking lots . . . you get the picture. He also devised his own craft beverage, the very drinkable Steve Austin's Broken Skull IPA. Yet, this beer-drinkin', ass-kickin' S.O.B. is actually something of a wine enthusiast, and he occasionally posts photos of his various trips to Napa Valley on his social media accounts.

In a 2018 interview with FOXSports.com, Austin recalled his WCW days traveling on the road and sharing the occasional bottle of red wine with legendary commentator Jim Ross. During a December 2014 interview with *Rolling Stone*, he labeled himself "a bit of a wine connoisseur" who over the years has transitioned from Napa Valley–based cabernets to pinot noirs.

Make no mistake, though: If beer and wine ever square off in the ring and Stone Cold is the referee, expect a heel turn from Austin, a steel chair to the bottled pinot, and a swig of beer for the working man. *Oh, hell yeah!*

STONE COLD'S FIRST WWE TITLE CHANGE

Less than 24 hours after Stone Cold won his first WWE Title at *WrestleMania XIV*, WWE Chairman Vince McMahon opened the March 30, 1998, edition of *Raw* to present The Texas Rattlesnake with a newly designed championship belt. Replacing Reggie Parks' "Winged Eagle" motif that had adorned the title since 1988, the new championship — designed by belt maker Joe Marshall — sported a blue leather strap and a "Big Eagle" design that embodied WWE's bold Attitude Era. Whereas the previous championship read "WWE World Heavyweight Wrestling Champion," the new design abbreviated it to read simply "WWE Champion."

In true Stone Cold fashion, Austin quickly eyed the new title that was slung over Mr. McMahon's shoulder, then took it and dropped the now-obsolete championship on the WWE Chairman's foot. The strap color would eventually revert back to black, and the design would sport the WWE scratch logo later that year.

"Stunning" Steve Austin [voiceover]: Ladies and gentlemen, it's the world-renowned celebration of nostalgia, "A Flare for the Old"! Featuring the seven-, or eight-, or nine-time World Champion, The Nature Boy! And featuring his maid, Pâté! And now, The Nature Boy, and tonight's special guest: One half of the World Tag Team Champions, Hollywood Blond "Stunning" Steve Austin!

"Flyin'" Brian Pillman [as a very old, cane-walking, winded "Ric Flair"]: Thank you, thank you very much. I'm, ah, I'm very pleased to announce a special segment of, uh, "A Flare for the Old." Here we are . . . Nursing Home Paradise . . . live here on, uh, via Technicolor. And, I know, uh, before we go any farther, I'd like to [*sighs*] give that moment every red-blooded male in America wants, and, uh . . . That's right, take a deep breath. [*sighs*] Let's bring her out — Pâté the maid! [*Pâté twirls.*] There she is, there she is . . . Woo! Ho-ho-ho, oh, you sex kitten, you! That's one of the little perks, ah, of being host of the show.

I'm very pleased to announce my special guest: One half of the World Tag Team Champions, "Stunning" Steve Austin! Let's bring him out!

[*Austin shakes Pillman/Flair's hand; Pillman/Flair shakes in pain.*]

How are you, Steve? I'm told that, ah, you and your partner are doing some very, ah, tremendous things, uh. You, and, ah, "Stunning" Steve are just a tremendous combination.

Austin: *I'm* "Stunning" Steve.

"Flair": Um . . . what was that?

Austin [louder]: *I'M "Stunning" Steve!*

"Flair": Anyway, Steve, uh . . . Maybe tell all the great fans out there, ah . . . some of the great things that, uh, the Blonds are doing with this tag team.

Austin: Well, I feel like with a partner like "Flyin'" Brian, The Hollywood Blonds can go . . . [*Shakes dozing Pillman/Flair awake.*] The Hollywood Blonds can go as . . . [*Shakes dozing Pillman/Flair awake again.*] *Hey! Wake up!* The Hollywood Blonds can go as far as they want to in tag team wrestling.

"Flair": Pardon me, Steve, uh, I believe it's time for, uh, for my medication. If you can hold on one minute, please? Please hold the microphone for me. [*Hands Austin the mic, tries to open a medication bottle.*]

Austin: Let-let-let-let-let me do that. Here. Open up, open up! [*Opens Pillman/Flair's mouth, throws pills in his face.*] There you go . . .

"Flair": Ah, thank you very much. Uh, I suppose you're wonderin' about that medication. Well, it's all legal and prescribed, ah, and, ah, you know, a little nitro[glycerin], uh, for the Alzheimer's and, uh, I got some vitamin E in there too. You know what they say, ah . . . "Helps keep the ol' pencil sharp," ah . . .

Austin: I wouldn't know about problems like that, but what I do notice is that the set's the same, but your best friend, your right-hand stooge . . . [*Arn Anderson comes out.*] There's Mr. Stooge, right there. I gotta say, Double A, it's a shame that The Nature Boy has to suffer of old age like this. But I've gotta say, lookin' at that body . . . [*Eyes Anderson up and down.*] The last time I saw a body like that, it had an apple stuffed in its mouth and it was roastin' over an open flame!

"Stunning" Steve Austin, with "Flyin'" Brian Pillman as an old, withered "Ric Flair," addresses Arn Anderson during The Hollywood Blonds' "Flare for the Old" (*WCW Saturday Night*, June 5, 1993)

THE RINGMASTER'S RING DEBUT

Let's "bottom-line" the facts regarding The Ringmaster's actual WWE in-ring premiere. Some believe his first match was against Matt Hardy on *Raw* January 15, 1996. Others contend his debut bout was against Scott Taylor, later known as Scotty 2 Hotty, on *Superstars of Wrestling* January 20, 1996.

In his 2003 autobiography, *The Stone Cold Truth*, Steve Austin cited the match with Taylor as The Ringmaster's first contest. The *correct* truth, however, is that he faced off against Matt Hardy.

The January 8 and January 15 editions of *Raw*, which featured The Ringmaster's debut and his match with Hardy, respectively, were both pre-recorded at the Bob Carpenter Center in Newark, DE, on December 18, 1995. Taylor squared off with The Million Dollar Man's handpicked champion during a *Superstars of Wrestling* taping at the Stabler Arena in Bethlehem, PA, on December *19*, 1995.

And *that's* the bottom line, because this book said so!

COLLEGE GRADUATE. ALMOST.

When Steve Williams's college football eligibility was up, he didn't have enough credits to graduate from the University of North Texas. To pay for an additional semester, he took a job working on a freight dock, but even that wasn't enough. The future Stone Cold Steve Austin left UNT only 17 hours short of graduating with a college diploma. He has never regretted his decision.

AN AUSTIN-ROCK ANGLE

Stone Cold Steve Austin became only the second Superstar to win six WWE Championships after beating Kurt Angle on *Raw* October 8, 2001. The only man who achieved that milestone before Austin was The Rock, who won his sixth WWE Title over seven months earlier at *No Way Out* . . . by defeating Kurt Angle.

On the other hand, at least Angle can claim he won his first two WWE Championships against The Great One and The Texas Rattlesnake.

AUSTIN IN ECW? JESUS CHRIST ...

S teve Austin went from "Stunning" to "The Extreme Superstar" when he joined Extreme Championship Wrestling (ECW) in fall 1995. To exemplify his updated moniker and new, unreserved persona, Austin headed ringside to a 20th anniversary London cast recording of "Superstar," the title song to Andrew Lloyd Webber and Tim Rice's iconic rock opera, *Jesus Christ Superstar*.

BRAWL IN THE FAMILY?

N early 68,000 in Houston's Reliant Astrodome were stridently divided over who to cheer for in Stone Cold Steve Austin and The Rock's No Disqualification Match for the WWE Championship at *WrestleMania X-Seven*. According to Austin, two WWE Universe attendees were particularly vocal and got "into an exchange." Stone Cold's brother, Kevin Williams, cussed and roared for his sibling to kick The Rock's ass. This drew the ire of The Great One's mother, Ata Johnson, who was seated nearby. Williams told Johnson to turn back around and watch the match. *Ouch.*

Fortunately, when Austin and The Rock's families met up at WWE's post-*WrestleMania* party, everyone, including Williams and Johnson, got along fine. No one ate a Stone Cold Stunner or Rock Bottom during the festivities.

WHO THREW HIM ALL THAT BEER?

After a match, Stone Cold Steve Austin often celebrated with the WWE Universe by hoisting and bashing together cans of Steveweisers inside the ring. But he needed someone to throw him the beer. During his 29 years with WWE, Mark Yeaton refereed matches, set up rings, and rang the bell as the company's timekeeper. You'll find him showing up in huge moments throughout WWE history, including helping to break up the melee that ensued between Mr. T and "Rowdy" Roddy Piper at *WrestleMania 2*. Yet, his greatest job — at least in Stone Cold's eyes — was tossing cans of beer to the Rattlesnake with uncanny pinpoint accuracy.

"Vince, let's cut through all the B.S. I know for a fact that you hate me. But that's okay. That's okay because I hate you right back. What you've gotta understand is there ain't gonna be no 'you and me.' There ain't no 'we.' You ain't gonna mold me, you ain't gonna break me. What you see, Vince, is what you get, and if you don't like that, tough luck!"

The new WWE Champion responds to Mr. McMahon's advice to do things "the easy way" and "learn to be flexible" . . . then Stunners him (*Raw*, March 30, 1998)

A RECORD AUSTIN WILL NEVER BREAK

In a September 2016 interview with *Louder*, Stone Cold Steve Austin discussed ten albums that changed his life. Though the interview is focused primarily on classic rock and metal, The Texas Rattlesnake revealed that the first album he ever purchased was Earth, Wind & Fire's *The Best of Earth, Wind & Fire, Vol. 1*. He bought it primarily for the legendary band's cover of "Got to Get You Into My Life," made by the equally-if-not-more legendary band, The Beatles.

AUSTIN LOVES A "PARADE"

Steve Austin had put his Ringmaster gimmick in the rearview mirror, but Stone Cold wanted innovative entrance music to drive home his new in-ring persona. With that, he gave WWE composer Jim Johnston a copy of "Bulls on Parade" by Rage Against the Machine. After listening to the song, Johnston started playing notes on his guitar and, inspired to open with the amalgamated sound of two glass breaks, an explosion, and a car crash, wrote "Hell Frozen Over" in 20 minutes.

On October 20, 1996, at *In Your House: Buried Alive*, the sound of glass shattering echoed in the Market Square Arena in

Indianapolis, IN, and "Hell Frozen Over" played for the first time as Stone Cold headed to the ring for his first pay-per-view match against Triple H.

AUSTIN'S HEART SCARE

On March 30, 2003, the world didn't realize that Stone Cold's *WrestleMania XIX* match against The Rock was also his in-ring curtain call. Neither did anyone realize that Steve Austin very nearly didn't make it to The Showcase of the Immortals that night in Seattle's Safeco Field.

Twenty-four hours earlier, Austin, who was already feeling "off" over the past few days, experienced what he thought was the onset of a heart attack. Rushed from his hotel room to a nearby hospital, it was determined that he had been suffering from severe dehydration, brought on by drinking up to two pots of coffee and five energy drinks with Ephedra daily for months. The hospital pumped Austin full of IV fluid and discharged him the following morning, and he somehow managed to engage in another classic confrontation with The Great One that evening at The Show of Shows.

HOW VAN HALEN SAVED HIS CAREER

Steve Austin had three entrance themes during his time with WCCW and USWA. When he started out as a good guy in 1989, he'd head ringside to "a symphony of silence" in Memphis's Mid-South Coliseum. Knowing that having no entrance music might kill his career before it could take off, he convinced the promotion to let him come out to Van Halen's "Unchained."

When Austin turned into an antagonist around 1990, he used "Fame" by David Bowie before going with another Van Halen classic, "Runnin' with the Devil," when his "Student vs. Teacher" rivalry with mentor "Gentleman" Chris Adams intensified.

NEVER COUNT HIM OUT

In its 33-year history, Stone Cold Steve Austin remains the only WWE Superstar to win a Royal Rumble Match after technically being eliminated. It occurred during the 1997 installment of the 30-man, over-the-top-rope extravaganza. Bret Hart had tossed Austin over, but the referees outside the ring were distracted, giving the Rattlesnake time to climb back in and eliminate the Hit Man.

A FACE MADE FOR TV (GUIDE)

Years ago, gracing the cover of a *TV Guide* was a significant indicator that you were on top of the entertainment world. The Texas Rattlesnake accomplished that feat *twice* within a four-month period. Stone Cold Steve Austin covered the December 5, 1998, and March 27, 1999, editions of the magazine. A publishing juggernaut, *TV Guide* boasted a circulation of nearly 12 million subscribers at the time, the largest for any publication in the United States.

If that wasn't enough, between those two editions, the Canadian version of *TV Guide* tapped Austin for its February 6, 1999, cover. In terms of popularity, Stone Cold, *Monday Night Raw*, and WWE's Attitude Era were at their hell-raising zenith.

0:49

"You can damn well bet [13's] gonna be an unlucky
number for Bret Hart! But let me just say this:
A Submission Match is not my kind of match. Do I
know a whole lot of wrestling holds? *Hell no, I don't!*
But I'll beat the hell out of ya till you do say, 'I quit!'

"You sit there, every time you get on TV, and say you been
screwed. Let me just tell you this, son: I ain't bringin' a
condom to the ring. *I'm bringin' a hell of a can of whoop-ass!*"

Stone Cold Steve Austin's message to Bret "Hit
Man" Hart before their Submission Match
at *WrestleMania 13* (March 23, 1997)

WINNING WITH CONSISTENCY

Stone Cold won all six of his WWE Championships at either The Showcase of the Immortals or on Monday night WWE programming. He captured three of his WWE Titles at *WrestleMania XIV* (March 29, 1998), *XV* (March 28, 1999), and *X-Seven* (April 1, 2001), respectively, and the other three on episodes of *Raw* (June 29, 1998, June 28, 1999, and October 8, 2001).

THE STUNNER HEARD 'ROUND THE WORLD

"I appreciate the fact that you and the [WWE] care. And I also appreciate the fact that, hell, you can kiss my ass!"

September 22, 1997, marked the inaugural *Monday Night Raw* to emanate from New York City's Madison Square Garden. And there was no place better for Steve Austin to deliver his first-ever Stone Cold Stunner to Vince McMahon.

McMahon had tried reasoning with Austin, who persisted in attacking Owen Hart, even though he had a restraining order against him and he still wasn't medically cleared after suffering his neck injury at *SummerSlam*. But the Rattlesnake wasn't having any of it. He simply ended the conversation with a Stunner,

was arrested and taken to jail, and in the progress ignited a storied rivalry with WWE's Chairman.

BLACK TIE UNFAIR

Steve Austin is unbeaten in Tuxedo Matches. Yes, you read that right.

Stone Cold wouldn't have been caught dead wearing a tuxedo on *Raw*. "Stunning" Steve, on the other hand, actually requested that he and Johnny B. Badd don "penguin suits" when they were given the opportunity to square off and tear off in a "dream match" of their choosing on *WCW Worldwide*, May 7, 1994. (Badd had unsuccessfully lobbied for a Boxing Match, which would have played to his strength as a Golden Gloves pugilist.)

Austin's WCW United States Heavyweight Title wasn't on the line that night, but he could have used the support to help prevent Badd from tearing away at his tux. He was fortunate that Colonel Robert Parker pulled down what remained of Badd's pants while Austin distracted the referee. "Stunning" Steve then quickly made it seem as if he had pulled apart the rest of Badd's tuxedo. It wasn't a classy move, but it gave him the win.

DAME 3:16

W hen the Portland Trail Blazers turned a home pregame into a Halloween party in October 2018, All-Star point guard Damian Lillard rolled into the Moda Center tricked out as Stone Cold Steve Austin, complete with an Austin mask and 3:16 T-shirt, and carrying a replica Smoking Skull WWE Championship.

"Big Game Dame" then took his fandom to another level in January 2020; with Austin and WWE's blessing, he and Adidas unveiled a Stone Cold colorway of his signature sneaker, the Dame 6. All-black uppers embody the signature "Austin 3:16" shirt, while metallic gold accents represent Stone Cold's championship pedigree. There's also embossed leather made to resemble snakeskin, insoles accented by a skull graphic, and a black caution tape effect that spells out "DAME 3:16" on the medial heel insole. The bottom line about this sneaker is that it's a ballin' "heel turn" guaranteed to appeal to Austin enthusiasts.

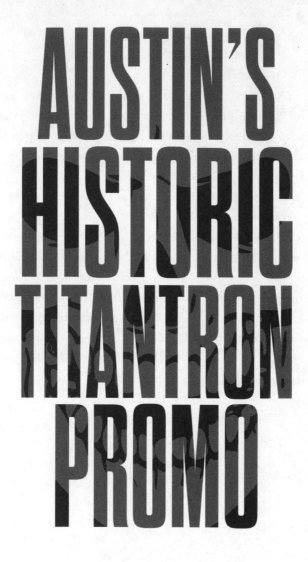

AUSTIN'S HISTORIC TITANTRON PROMO

"Shut your hole, Shamrock! Just shut your hole, son. Because you can sit there and say it's an honor for you to be a part of *WrestleMania 13*. You ought to consider it an honor I don't come out there and stomp your little guts in right now!"

Stone Cold addresses Ken Shamrock in the first promo exchange between one Superstar on the TitanTron and another inside the ring (*Raw*, March 10, 1997)

A LESS-THAN-SATISFYING VICTORY

W inning your first WWE Championship on The Grandest Stage of Them All should thrill just about anyone with a dream or interest of becoming a sports entertainer. For Steve Austin, claiming his first WWE Title at *WrestleMania XIV* was . . . disappointing. During a January 2015 edition of *The Steve Austin Show*, Austin recalled being happy about winning the title, but he told Vince McMahon afterward that he thought his bout with Shawn Michaels was "the drizzling sh*ts."

Both Austin and Michaels were battling injuries going into the contest, and The Showstopper, as Austin described on his podcast, "wasn't in a good place, physically or mentally." HBK had suffered a severe back injury at *Royal Rumble* two months earlier, and he had developed a serious chip on his shoulder about dropping the championship at The Show of Shows. As Michaels and Austin would discuss, it wasn't so much the idea of losing to the white-hot Stone Cold that upset HBK as it was the prospect of his career ending with that match.

McMahon told Austin not to worry about it, for the real fun would begin that Monday night on *Raw*. To paraphrase Jim Ross at the end of *WrestleMania XIV*, the Austin era had begun.

FIRST TASTE OF CHAMPIONSHIP GOLD

Championship gold followed Steve Austin early in his career. On November 10, 1990, he and "California Stud" Rod Price defeated The Angel of Death & Abdullah the Butcher in the Dallas Sportatorium to capture the Texas Wrestling Federation (TWF) Tag Team Titles.

Austin and Price's tag title reign was short-lived, however; the titles were abandoned when the TWF promotion folded in May 1991. Nevertheless, it was the first of many championships that the WWE Hall of Famer would hold.

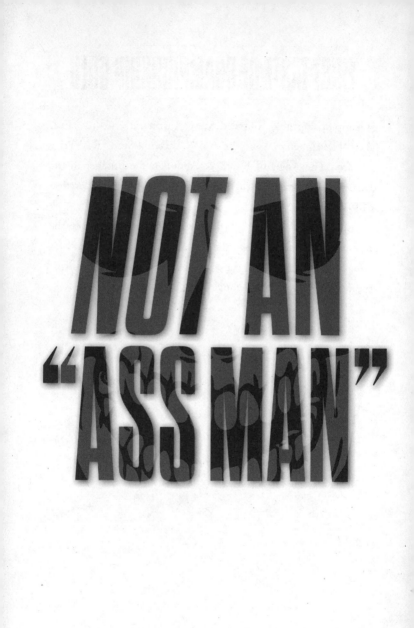

0:57

"As far as 'Bad Ass' Billy Gunn goes, someone said, 'Hey, Stone Cold — do you got a match?' I said, 'Oh, hell yeah, I got a match: *My foot in Billy Gunn's ass!*' So hit his damn music to bring his little carcass to the ring!"

Stone Cold Steve Austin calls out "Bad Ass" Billy Gunn (*Raw*, November 1, 1999)

"LIKE IT OR NOT, YOU'RE A GOOD GUY"

In the buildup to *WrestleMania 13*, sentiment toward Bret Hart and Steve Austin was drastically changing. The hero was turning into the villain, and vice versa. The problem was, Austin wasn't trying to become a protagonist, nor did he want to. He believed that WWE Superstars who broke the rules had much more creative liberty with their personas and their actions. Stone Cold eventually changed his mind when Jim Ross showed him sales numbers that proved how much good guys' T-shirts outperformed those belonging to bad guys. He agreed to what ultimately became a double switch at The Showcase of the Immortals, so long as he didn't have to adjust his in-ring style.

RIGHT TO CENSOR?

Despite gaining the WWE Universe's attention with his "Austin 3:16" speech at *King of the Ring*, Stone Cold Steve Austin wasn't quite yet allowed to cut loose. The Rattlesnake learned that after noticing that his verbal browbeating of Aldo Montoya and his "jockstrap" of a mask had been heavily edited for television. When Austin asked Vince McMahon why, the WWE Chairman explained that Stone Cold's promos had been making people back at the studio laugh out loud. Because Austin was supposed to be a bad guy, WWE management wanted to make sure that fans didn't like him.

The Rattlesnake argued that his personality was the one thing that enabled him to compete with anyone in WWE, especially the larger, bulkier WWE Superstars whose stature he couldn't physically match. Austin credits McMahon for listening and pulling back on the promo edits, which gave Stone Cold the biggest advantage he needed in the ring.

0:60

BLOOD FROM A STONE COLD

Steve Austin went through a particularly rough stretch going into and heading out of Pittsburgh, PA's Civic Center for *King of the Ring* on June 28, 1998. Stone Cold certainly lived up to his reputation as The Toughest S.O.B. in WWE, making the event despite being hospitalized inside Houston's Hermann Hospital for more than three days with a 104-degree fever brought on by a severe staph infection in his right elbow.

Next, early into his First Blood Match title defense against Kane, Austin developed a minor cut on his back. Fortunately, referee Earl Hebner had stated during the pay-per-view's pre-show that he wouldn't end the match due to minor scratches. Unfortunately for Austin, it only delayed the inevitable — he'd bleed crimson after Undertaker's accidental chair blast busted him open and cost him his first WWE Title reign.

TAG TEAM GLORY JUST OUT OF REACH

Eight months before he and "Flyin'" Brian Pillman won the unified WCW/NWA World Tag Team Championship, "Stunning" Steve Austin was in the running for one of those tandem titles with his Dangerous Alliance cohort, WCW United States Heavyweight Champion Rick Rude. The duo competed in a tournament for the NWA World Tag Team Championship, and advanced past the first round with a victory over "The Z-Man," Tom Zenk & Marcus Alexander Bagwell at *Clash of the Champions XIX* (June 22, 1992). They weren't so successful during the quarter-final round at *The Great American Bash* in Georgia's Albany Civic Center (July 12, 1992), when Austin & Rude lost to Dustin Rhodes & Barry Windham.

Oddly enough, Austin's namesake, "Dr. Death" Steve Williams, went on to win the NWA World Tag Team Championship with his Miracle Violence Connection partner, Terry "Bam Bam" Gordy. In doing so, they also unified that title with the WCW World Tag Team Championship, which they won from the Steiner Brothers one week earlier.

AUSTIN VS. UNDERTAKER
... KIND OF ...

The Texas Rattlesnake and The Phenom share a long history that actually dates back long before the dawn of WWE's Attitude Era. Stone Cold Steve Austin and Undertaker first battled in the Dallas Sportatorium on the November 4, 1989, edition of *USWA Challenge*. Austin, however, wrestled under his given name, Steve Williams, while Undertaker was "The Punisher," a masked master of inflicting pain. Unlike their brutal melees years later at WWE, this contest was short-lived and relatively one-sided in The Punisher's favor.

In January 1990, the two clashed again at a few events in Memphis's Mid-South Coliseum, where the newly rechristened Steve *Austin* gained a measure of retribution against The Punisher in tag team action. Each had paired with other future WWE alumni — Austin partnered with Dutch Mantell (Uncle Zebekiah, Zeb Colter), the man who came up with his new surname. The Punisher, meanwhile, teamed with The Soultaker, whom the WWE Universe more fondly remembers as Papa Shango, Kama Mustafa, or The Godfather.

THE KING OF IMPROV

Those who watched *King of the Ring* in 1996 might think that Stone Cold Steve Austin had prepared his iconic "Austin 3:16" promo hours, if not days, in advance. The truth is his words were unscripted and completely adlibbed.

During his tournament semi-final match with Marc Mero, Austin took a kick to the mouth that required him to leave Milwaukee's MECCA Arena and get his lacerated upper lip stitched up at a nearby emergency room. He returned to the arena just after Jake "The Snake" Roberts defeated Vader in their match, and Michael P.S. Hayes informed The Texas Rattlesnake that Roberts had cut a religious-based promo about him. Hearing that made Austin think about football fans in the end zone holding up "John 3:16" signs during extra point attempts, and it gave him an idea.

After Austin defeated Roberts in the finals to win the King of the Ring Tournament, no one really knew what he intended to say. When Dok Hendrix (Hayes) game him the microphone, out came "Austin 3:16," as well as another of his most popular catchphrases: "And that's the bottom line, 'cause Stone Cold said so!"

POLITICAL STUNNERS

I f you think politicians are exempt from receiving a Stone Cold Stunner, think again.

To be clear, no one actually held a public office when Stone Cold Steve Austin hit them with his finisher. Several years after feeling The Texas Rattlesnake's bite, however, these three individuals took on prominent roles within the United States government:

- **Kane:** The Big Red Monster ate more Stunners than anyone in this select group, but he also defeated Stone Cold for the WWE Championship in June 1998. In August 2018, Kane — aka Glenn Jacobs — won his bid to become Mayor of Knox County, TN.

- **Linda McMahon:** Though she arguably drew Austin's in-ring ire less than any of the McMahon family, she more than earned a Stunner during the *Raw* Homecoming on October 3, 2005. Years after stepping away from her duties as CEO of WWE, McMahon was confirmed as administrator of the Small Business Administration in February 2017. In April 2019, she was named Chairwoman of America First Action.

- **Donald Trump:** Austin was the special guest referee for "The Donald" and Mr. McMahon's heated "Battle of the Billionaires" at *WrestleMania 23*, where each magnate had a Superstar represent them in the ring and the loser of the match would have his head shaved bald. Long story short, Trump persevered, McMahon was sheared, and both billionaires bought a Stone Cold Stunner for their trouble. On November 8, 2016, Trump was elected as the 45th president of the United States.

A few other WWE Superstars have made unsuccessful bids to hold public office, including Jerry "The King" Lawler and Rhyno. Stone Cold also hit them with Stunners. He's an equal opportunity hellraiser.

"You come out here and you start asking all these stupid questions. You know, what we do . . . it's none of your business. It's none of these people's business. But . . . when the time's right, we'll let you know, honey. As far as I'm concerned, this interview is *over*."

"Stunning" Steve Austin (with Vivacious Veronica) keeps Missy Hyatt's interview short and not-so-sweet in his first World Championship Wrestling appearance (*WCW Saturday Night*, May 25, 1991)

AUSTIN'S ANIMATED ADVENTURES

Long before his animated appearances on *WWE Story Time* and *Camp WWE*, The Texas Rattlesnake had a history of being drawn to the cartoon world. From 1998 until 2002, Stone Cold lent his voice to MTV's popular *Celebrity Deathmatch*, a cacophony of claymation clashes between celebrities from all walks of life. Whether he competed in bouts or served as a guest commentator, Austin had no problem mixing it up whenever referee Mills Lane urged fighters, "Let's get it on!"

It's possible Austin took a cue from Lane, Nevada's most outspoken judge, when he appeared as one on Scott Adams's comic strip-turned-animated series *Dilbert*. On the June 13, 2000, episode "The Delivery," Judge Stone Cold Steve Austin made a *WrestleMania 13*–worthy entrance into the courtroom, hit a reporter with the Stone Cold Stunner, and bashed beers at the bench before presiding.

SELF-MADE REDNECK

Though Steve Austin credits WWE Hall of Fame commentator Jim Ross for coming up with several of his monikers and signature moves, "The Bionic Redneck" came from ol' Stone Cold himself. Austin stated on several occasions that the gimmick originated simply due to years of wear and tear on his body. He has a right arm that to this day won't straighten out and plates in his neck, and he eventually took to wearing double knee braces to deal with torn PCLs and ACLs.

As he explained in a 2017 episode of his podcast *The Steve Austin Show*, the internal and external hardware "became part of [my] ring gear . . . It was a very interesting look. It looked like I was ready to go in there and go to battle, stomp a mudhole in somebody's ass, and walk it dry."

0:68

TEXAS-BRED WWE HALL OF FAMERS

In 2009, Stone Cold Austin became the sixth Texan inducted into WWE's Hall of Fame. As of December 2020, 24 of the Hall's 210 inductees were raised in the Lone Star State. (This includes two Legacy Wing inductees and Shawn Michaels, who was born in Chandler, AZ, but raised in San Antonio, TX.)

- Tito Santana (2004)
- Eddie Guerrero (2006)
- Blackjack Lanza (2006)
- Blackjack Mulligan (2006)
- Dusty Rhodes (2007)
- Stone Cold Steve Austin (2009)
- Dory Funk Jr. (2009)
- Terry Funk (2009)
- Von Erich Family — David, Kevin, Kerry, Fritz, Mike, and Chris (2009)
- Ted DiBiase (2010)

- Wendi Richter (2010)
- Shawn Michaels (2011, 2019)
- Tully Blanchard (2012)
- Barry Windham (2012)
- Booker T (2013, 2019)
- Jake "The Snake" Roberts (2014)
- Big Boss Man (2016)
- Stan Hansen (2016)
- Jacqueline (2016)
- June Byers (2017, Legacy Wing inductee)
- Haystacks Calhoun (2017, Legacy Wing inductee)
- Mark Henry (2018)
- Stevie Ray (2019)
- John Bradshaw Layfield (2020)

HISTORIC ENTRY, FAST EXIT

On January 24, 1999, Chyna made history as the first female to enter the 30-Superstar Royal Rumble Match. The Ninth Wonder of the World managed to eliminate The World's Strongest Man, Mark Henry, before she was tossed over the top rope and onto the outside floor. And the WWE Superstar responsible for her exit was none other than Stone Cold Steve Austin.

Ironically, it was also The Bionic Redneck who helped Chyna achieve her sports-entertainment milestone. Two weeks earlier on *Raw*, he disrupted Mr. McMahon's "Corporate Royal Rumble" long enough for her to secure the No. 30 entrant spot into the Royal Rumble Match.

In addition to eliminating the first female competitor in Royal Rumble history, Austin was the first No. 1 entrant to oust a No. 30 entrant. That wouldn't happen again until 2018, when Sasha Banks eliminated Trish Stratus in the inaugural Women's Royal Rumble Match.

0:70

ICE WATER IN HIS VEINS

On *Raw* March 11, 1996, though he still had the Million Dollar Championship and Ted DiBiase as his manager, The Ringmaster was officially announced as Stone Cold Steve Austin. He battled Savio Vega to a double-countout.

Technically, though, Austin's first match as Stone Cold took place in Corpus Christi, TX, on March *10*, when he defeated Aldo Montoya during a taping for the March 16 edition of *Superstars of Wrestling*. This taping also featured a budding young prospect in his first WWE dark match, where he picked up the victory against The Brooklyn Brawler. The newcomer's name? Dwayne Johnson, aka Rocky Maivia, aka The Rock.

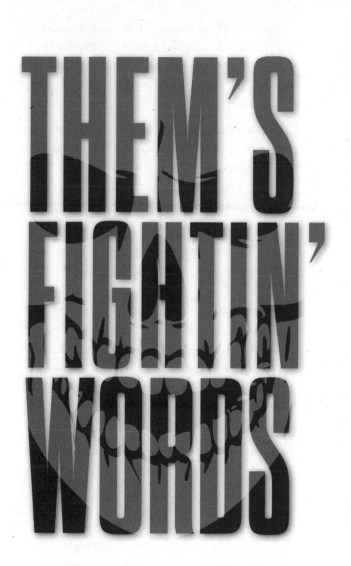

"I am sick and tired of seein' Mike Tyson. He comes in, he's shakin' everybody's hands, makin' friends with all the [WWE] Superstars, and it's made me so damn sick I've been in the back throwin' up!

"I ain't gonna shake your damn hand, because I ain't out here to make friends with ya. Mike . . . I respect what you done in the boxing world, but Jesus Christ, son, when you step in this ring, you're messin' with Stone Cold Steve Austin, and that's something you *don't* do!

"Let me make it short and sweet: What I'm tellin' you is *I want a piece of Mike Tyson's ass!*

"I respect what you done, Mike, but you're out here callin' yourself 'The Baddest Man on the Planet.' Right now, you've got your beady little eyes locked on the eyes of *the world's toughest son of a bitch*! I can beat you any day of the week, twice on Sunday.

"Do I think you can beat my ass? Hell, no! Do I think I can beat your ass? Why, *hell yeah*! I don't know how good your hearing is, but if you don't understand what I'm sayin', I always got a little bit of sign language, so here's to ya!" [*Flips both middle fingers in Tyson's face.*]

Stone Cold interrupts Vince McMahon's announcement regarding *WrestleMania XIV* and "Iron" Mike Tyson (*Raw*, January 19, 1998)

HE DIDN'T SIGN UP FOR THIS

Before John Cena enlisted for his first starring film role in *The Marine*, WWE Studios (then called WWE Films) tried recruiting Stone Cold Steve Austin for the action vehicle. Austin declined after reading the script about a discharged marine who must rescue his kidnapped wife from a murderous gang of thieves. Instead, he opted to star in the studio's *The Condemned*, and play a death row inmate who's forced to compete in an illegally broadcast game of survival against other lethal criminals on a deserted island.

The Texas Rattlesnake didn't reprise his 2007 role for *The Condemned 2*, so WWE Studios tapped another serpentine Superstar for the 2015 sequel: The Viper, Randy Orton.

SLAMMY AWARD WINNER

Two days before *WrestleMania 13*, USA Network broadcast the 1997 Slammy Awards live. Nominated for seven awards, Stone Cold Steve Austin won The Larry Flynt Freedom of Speech Slammy, beating out Jerry "The King" Lawler, Paul E. Dangerously, Faarooq, and radio shock-jock Howard Stern. And there was anything but gratitude in the tuxedoed Rattlesnake's acceptance speech:

"I've been instructed we're runnin' short on time, so I'll go ahead and bottom-line it. When some people think of pro wrestlin', they get a little snicker in their voice and a little smile on their face. In my mind, I think of blood, sweat, and tears. At *WrestleMania 13*, Bret Hart, don't expect any less from me, 'cause that's *exactly* what I expect from you. At *WrestleMania 13*, son, any way it goes, it will be a hell of a fight . . . and it will never be over. Not ever, Bret. Not until your ass goes back to Calgary and sits on the couch and watches Stone Cold [on *Raw*] every Monday night!"

Austin then proceeded to open up a can of whoop-ass on Doink the Clown, who had been heckling him before his speech.

The WWE Hall of Famer would win his next Slammy 18 years later, when his *Stone Cold Podcast* garnered enough votes through WWE's social media accounts to earn Best Original WWE Network Show.

0:74

TELEVISION STAYING POWER

"**S**tunning" Steve Austin was the longest reigning WCW World Television Champion of the modern era. After winning the title from "Beautiful" Bobby Eaton on June 3, 1991 (aired on *WCW World Wide Wrestling*, June 29), he successfully defended it for 329 days. Austin's reign officially ended on April 27, 1992 (aired on *WCW Saturday Night*, May 9), when he lost the title to Barry Windham in a Two Out of Three Falls thriller. The statistic holds even if you go by the airdates, which put the reign at 315 days.

Before the championship had been renamed under the WCW brand, only NWA Television Champions Paul Jones (NWA Television Champion, 368 days) and Tully Blanchard (353 days), plus NWA World Television Champions Arn Anderson (336 days) and Mike Rotunda (335 days), had surpassed Austin's first reign.

A month after losing the WCW World Television Championship, Austin won the title back from Windham and held on to it for another 102 days.

0:75

ORIGIN OF THE STONE COLD STUNNER

S teve Austin has long credited Fabulous Freebird Michael P.S. Hayes with teaching him the Stone Cold Stunner. Austin was still ironing out his Stone Cold character on Memorial Day in 1996 when Hayes approached him at a *Raw* taping in Fayetteville, NC. It was there that Hayes told him about the Ace Crusher, a move used in Japan by Johnny Ace (aka WWE SVP of Talent Relations and onetime *Raw* General Manager John Laurinaitis).

After slightly modifying the Ace Crusher by doing it from a sit-down position, Austin practiced the move with several local talent before he used it during the *Raw* taping, in a King of the

Ring quarter-finals match against Savio Vega. The finisher didn't have a name until announcer Jim Ross later called it the Stone Cold Stunner. Austin has admitted in interviews that he didn't like the name at first, but it quickly grew on him and the WWE Universe.

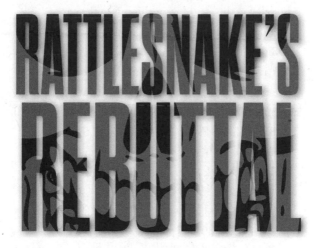

"I'll tell you this, and I want this put in the contract . . .
Bret Hart says if he gets beat, he won't wrestle in the
United States again. *Big deal!* If I cannot beat Owen
Hart at *SummerSlam*, after the match, when he pins me
one-two-three — *if* that happens — he can pull down
his trunks, pull down his little panties, bend over, and I'll
kiss him right on his ass, right in front of the world! Put
that in the contract. That's the bottom line. I'll kiss his
ass if I can't kick it, and that's the way it's gonna be!"

Stone Cold ups the ante on his Intercontinental
Title Match with champion Owen Hart at
SummerSlam (*Raw*, July 7, 1997)

"IT'S A CHOPPER, BABY."

Steve Austin competed in WCCW, USWA, and WCW with a full head of (sometimes long) flowing, blond hair. He realized for some time, however, that it was thinning out, and he once visited a local Hair Club for Men in Atlanta, GA. The experience completely turned Austin off the idea of a hair transplant, so before he started at WWE in late 1995, he went with "Plan B": Rocking a buzzcut that was inspired by Butch Coolidge, the character played by Bruce Willis in *Pulp Fiction*.

When Austin's Ringmaster gimmick went (stone) cold, he eventually convinced WWE to change his moniker and persona. Yet it took further inspiration from Mickey Knox, the hairless predator portrayed by Woody Harrelson in *Natural Born Killers*, to prompt Austin into shaving his head completely bald and growing out facial hair. The WWE Hall of Famer recalled on an episode of the WWE Network series *WWE Story Time* that the head-shaving process started, rather suitably, while he was in Pittsburgh, PA, for a WWE live event at the *Mellon* Arena.

DESIGNATED FOR ASSIGNMENT

Long before the beer-swiggin' hellraiser double-fisted Steve-weisers inside a WWE ring or crafted his Broken Skull IPA, Steve Austin was considered the most responsible of the four Williams brothers growing up in Edna, Texas. When his siblings and their buddies wanted to buy six-packs and go partying, Austin was the designated driver, chauffeuring them around in his mother's car. He was, as he described in his 2003 autobiography *The Stone Cold Truth*, "a big-ass babysitter."

A PAY-PER-VIEW MUST-SEE

"Stunning" Steve Austin competed in 24 matches at WCW pay-per-view events and two with Extreme Championship Wrestling. Of those pay-per-views, Austin factored into the main event on three occasions. Stone Cold Steve Austin, on the other hand, competed 70 times in WWE pay-per-views, more than twice the amount of WCW and ECW combined. He main-evented 42 of those pay-per-views.

These numbers include matches where Austin wrestled twice at a pay-per-view, both *In Your House: Beware of Dog* Strap Matches and his U.K.-exclusive pay-per-view bouts. They do not include dark matches, with the exception of *SummerSlam* in 1996, when his match with Yokozuna was part of the "Free-For-All" before the pay-per-view.

STONE COLD BEER BASH

May 5, 2003, was a very productive first *Raw* for its new Co-General Manager, Stone Cold Steve Austin. Inside the Metro Centre in Halifax, Nova Scotia, he righted a lot of wrongs previously committed by Eric Bischoff. That included rehiring Jim Ross as *Raw*'s announcer and reinstating the Intercontinental Title seven months after Bischoff had deactivated it.

If that wasn't already enough, Austin also declared a Stone Cold Beer Bash for later that evening, and he didn't disappoint. At the end of *Raw*, he celebrated with Goldberg while members of the WWE Universe and stadium vendors with trays of beer surrounded the ring. Molson, one of WWE's Canadian sponsors, was kind enough to deliver more than 40 cases of its Molson Canadian Export Ale, and Stone Cold put all of it to good use — so much, in fact, that he jokingly swam on a beer-soaked canvas.

AUSTIN GOES TO "HELL"

On June 15, 1998, Stone Cold & Undertaker battled Kane & Mankind in not only the first-ever Hell in a Cell Match on *Raw*, but also the first Tornado Tag Team Hell in a Cell Match. The hellacious bout officially ended as a No Contest, but after *Raw* went off the air, the Rattlesnake struck down Mankind with the Stone Cold Stunner to pick up a pinfall victory.

Undertaker and Mankind re-entered the steel structure only 13 days later at *King of the Ring*, in what was arguably the most iconic Hell in a Cell Match in sports-entertainment history.

0:82

"A *November to Remember*, son, is the debut of Steve Austin, because that clumsy-ass Sandman couldn't make it to the damn ring! I done told you once, you don't even deserve to be in the ring with me, not even the same damn building! You can get your ass out of the ring while he announces my name, because my name is Steve Austin, and tonight, for a very, very short while, your name is Eric Bischoff!"

"The Extreme Superstar" Steve Austin dispatches Sandman and makes himself ECW World Heavyweight Champion Mikey Whipwreck's new challenger at *November to Remember* (November 18, 1995)

THE TOUGHEST S.O.B. IN PODCASTING

Having conquered sports entertainment, television, reality TV, and film, Steve Austin ventured into a new career as a podcaster. On April 5, 2013, he launched *The Steve Austin Show* on PodcastOne, also a newcomer to the world of ad-supported, on-demand digital audio network. The show was an immediate success that fully realized Austin's versatility as a speaker, a storyteller, an interviewer, and a down-to-earth (albeit vocal) person splitting his time between living in Los Angeles and on his Broken Skull Ranch in Texas.

The Steve Austin Show quickly expanded from one to two episodes per week (including a decidedly un-PG, "Unleashed" version of the program), generating between a half million to more than one million downloads per episode. For 520 episodes, no topic was taboo and celebrities from all walks of life — including Austin's fellow sports entertainers, naturally — were welcome.

Austin's podcasting success made its way onto WWE Network in December 2014, when The Texas Rattlesnake hosted no-holds-barred interviews with WWE Superstars, starting with Vince McMahon, on *Stone Cold Podcast*. In November 2019, the successful format transitioned into a new talk show on the network, called *Steve Austin's Broken Skull Sessions*, which premiered with a rare interview with Undertaker.

FOR THE RECORD

On August 25, 1998, Mars Entertainment Corp. (known today as Spy Records) released *Steve Austin's Stone Cold Metal*, a 14-track compilation of rock music handpicked by The Texas Rattlesnake himself. Featuring a lenticular case that morphed Austin's head into a human skull, *Stone Cold Metal* became the first wrestling album to chart on the *Billboard* 200, debuting at No. 174 and selling 32,000 units its first week. The album spent four weeks on the *Billboard* 200 and peaked at No. 170.

Track listing:

- "Rock You Like a Hurricane" — Scorpions
- "God of Thunder" — KISS
- "Balls to the Wall" — Accept
- "Perfect Strangers" — Deep Purple
- "Breaking the Chains" — Dokken
- "Dreams I'll Never See" — Molly Hatchet
- "Stranglehold" — Ted Nugent
- "Detroit Rock City" — KISS
- "Rainbow in the Dark" — Dio
- "No One Like You" — Scorpions
- "Slow Ride" — Foghat
- "On Through the Night" — Def Leppard
- "Rain" — The Cult
- "Stone Cold" — Rainbow

CURTAIN RECALL

A Superstar on the rise was heavily favored to win the 1996 King of the Ring Tournament. It just wasn't Stone Cold Steve Austin.

Hunter Hearst Helmsley — who'd soon become far better known as Triple H — was WWE management's pick to be crowned in Milwaukee, WI, on June 23. But at a May 19 WWE live event at New York City's famed Madison Square Garden, Helmsley, WWE Champion Shawn Michaels, Diesel (Kevin Nash), and Razor Ramon (Scott Hall) converged inside the ring for the now-infamous "Curtain Call."

Though the four were close friends inside the WWE locker room — they were known as "The Kliq" — they each had rivalries with one another in the ring. With Nash and Hall leaving for WCW, the four Superstars broke character and embraced each other before a capacity crowd at MSG.

With Hall and Nash leaving and Michaels wearing the WWE Title, Helmsley bore the brunt of an internal reprimand. His planned push at *King of the Ring* was scrapped, and for much of the remaining year, he was either left off pay-per-view events or placed on the losing side of matches. Triple H more than made up for lost time when he won the tournament the following year and co-founded D-Generation X, while Austin 3:16 helped launch WWE's iconic Attitude Era.

STONE COLD'S LUKEWARM RECORD AGAINST THE HIT MAN

Stone Cold Steve Austin regards Bret Hart as one of his favorite opponents and someone instrumental to his WWE Hall of Fame career. Interestingly, despite all of his success against so many other Superstars, Austin has never pinned the Hit Man in a one-on-one encounter on WWE programming.

The Texas Rattlesnake fell to Hart in their very first televised match, *Sun City Superbowl*, an event that was broadcast in South Africa on September 14, 1996. He was on the losing side of their legendary skirmishes at *Survivor Series* and *WrestleMania 13*. In fact, his only victory in a pay-per-view match against Hart came via disqualification, at *In Your House: Revenge of the Taker* (April 20, 1997). Twenty-four hours after that encounter, the future WWE Hall of Famers clashed again in a Street Fight on *Raw*. The match ended in a No Contest, though Austin got the better of that exchange after beating the living hell out of Hart, both in the ring and in an ambulance that carted Hart away.

A SWEET RIDE

Back in his high school days in Edna, TX, Stone Cold Steve Austin didn't have a monster limo, beer truck, or Zamboni to ride around in. Instead, he saved up $1,500 doing odd jobs so that he could purchase his first car, a metallic brown 1971 Pontiac Formula Firebird. The vehicle's 455-cubic-inch V8 engine had been replaced with a Chevy 396, and features included a spoiler, a hood scoop with a white racing stripe running down the middle, and Cragar chrome Supersport mag wheels all the way around.

Austin admits that he used to think he had the finest-looking car in Edna, even though it turned out to be a pile of junk. Before long, he'd sell the Firebird and upgrade to a 1973 Chevy Camaro. The monster vehicles would follow soon enough.

TRULY SICK PERFORMANCES

Neither Stone Cold Steve Austin nor Undertaker were in peak condition while battling in the second-ever Buried Alive Match at *Rock Bottom: In Your House* (December 13, 1998). In addition to fighting a serious intestinal virus for nearly a month, The Texas Rattlesnake took a hard bump on the uneven dirt ground that injured an oblique and abdominal muscle early in the contest.

The Phenom wasn't faring much better; he was still nursing a broken ankle he had suffered at *King of the Ring* back in June.

Austin won the match, but he didn't waste much time celebrating. (Well, a little; he had some Steveweisers, and even tossed one into the grave for Undertaker.) Instead, he went straight to the hospital and missed appearing live on *Raw* for the remainder of the year.

0:89

"CALLING DR. AUSTIN"

Following a Zamboni-driving Stone Cold attack plus a Kane and Undertaker beatdown one week prior, Mr. McMahon tried convalescing in a hospital during *Raw* October 5, 1998. It didn't work out.

First, the Chairman received a visit from the sickeningly sweet Yurple the Clown and Mankind, who introduced McMahon (and the world) to his new pal, Mr. Socko. Soon after McMahon ordered them away and had his blood pressure checked, a doctor in scrubs said, "Oh, I'll take it from here, nurse." It was Steve Austin in disguise, and he administered 100 ccs of whoop-ass to the WWE Chairman. The Rattlesnake's treatment included pounding on McMahon's broken ankle, smacking him squarely in the skull with a five-pound bedpan, shocking him with defibrillator paddles, and ramming an enema where the sun doesn't shine. Mr. McMahon recovered physically, though the emotional scars no doubt remain.

WELCOME TO *REDNECK ISLAND*

I n June 2012, The Bionic Redneck forayed into reality television as the host of CMT's *Redneck Island*. Steve Austin divided 12 southern men and women — stereotyped as "rednecks" — to coexist as two teams on an uninhabited island and compete in physical and mental "Reckonings," or head-to-head challenges. The losing team for each week's Reckoning would vote one of its members off the island via a beer ballot. When only one contestant remained, they became the champion of Redneck Island and the recipient of $100,000 cash. Austin kept *Redneck Island* inhabited — and the rednecks in line — for five seasons on CMT.

Jim Ross: He is the perfect complement —

Mr. Perfect: Whoa, hold on there. What are you talking about, "perfect"? I'll admit he's close enough to perfect for me, Ross. But let *me* say the "perfect" part, will ya?

Vince McMahon: Well, he is definitely *stone cold*. Look at that demeanor, would you?

Commentators Jim Ross, Mr. Perfect, and Vince McMahon refer to a Stone Cold-esque Ringmaster as he sets to square off against Fatu, the Superstar who'd run him over with a car three years later as Rikishi (*Superstars of Wrestling*, February 10, 1996)

"IT'S A GREAT DAY TO BE A BLOND"

After WCW management decided to make a tag team out of "Stunning" Steve Austin and "Flyin'" Brian Pillman, the inexperienced tandem traveled together on the road and discussed new ideas with Scott Levy, who at the time ran in WCW as Scotty Flamingo. (He'd eventually undergo an Extreme makeover in ECW as Raven.) Austin remembers Levy suggesting that the duo call themselves The Hollywood Blonds, and they were off and running.

"AND THAT'S THE (ROCK) BOTTOM LINE . . ."

At *WrestleMania XV*, Stone Cold earned the distinction of being the first WWE Superstar to withstand The Rock's finisher, the Rock Bottom. The Rattlesnake defied the odds not only by kicking out of Rock's pinfall attempt, but also by rallying back from a second Rock Bottom and hitting The Great One with the Stone Cold Stunner to win his third WWE Championship.

THE RING MASTER BEFORE THE RINGMASTER

Steve Austin has gone on the record numerous times describing his original WWE character as "a suck-ass gimmick." Well, nearly three years before The Million Dollar Man, Ted DiBiase, introduced Austin to the WWE Universe as The Ringmaster, another WWE Superstar had been offered the name and persona.

Around April 1993, Bryan Clark turned down a concept for "The Ring Master," explaining that he didn't envision himself as an actual master of the ring. Instead, Clark opted to go with one of the other character designs WWE sent: The explosive behemoth known as Adam Bomb.

WHO REALLY WON THE AUSTIN-McMAHON WAR?

Incredible as it may seem, Vince — sorry, *Mr.* McMahon — has more victories over Stone Cold Steve Austin than Austin has over the WWE Chairman, and all of them happened in 1999. First, Mr. McMahon sent The Texas Rattlesnake over the top rope to win the 1999 Royal Rumble Match. On the February 8 edition of *Raw*, he pinned Austin, who had just endured a brutal Gauntlet Match beatdown from members of McMahon's Corporation. Last, the Chairman and Shane McMahon claimed Stone Cold's half-ownership of WWE after defeating him in a 2-on-1 Handicap Ladder Match at *King of the Ring* (June 27, 1999).

The Bionic Redneck's only competitive victory over his boss was arguably the most decisive one of their encounters. After the unexpected debut of Big Show, Austin literally escaped with the win in his one-on-one Steel Cage Match with McMahon at *St. Valentine's Day Massacre: In Your House* (February 14, 1999). Fortunately for the WWE Universe, he had already spent the entire bout beating the daylights out of the WWE Chairman.

AUSTIN'S MESSAGE FOR MANKIND

"DTA, you stupid piece of trash! Don't ever trust nobody! You ain't gonna be my partner, never, 'cause you're a long-haired freak and you suck!"

The Rattlesnake delivers a Stone Cold Stunner and some harsh words in response to Mankind's repeated requests to form a tag team (*Raw*, July 7, 1997)

AN EXTREME-LY SHORT STAY

"The Extreme Superstar" Steve Austin competed in just two matches during his tenure at Extreme Championship Wrestling (ECW), and both times for Mikey Whipwreck's ECW World Heavyweight Title. Austin ambushed and replaced an injured Sandman as challenger for the first title bout at *November to Remember* (November 18, 1995), though Whipwreck barely managed to retain the championship.

Whipwreck wasn't so fortunate when he, Austin, and Sandman clashed in a Three-Way Dance Match at *December to Dismember* (December 9, 1995). Austin caught the champion with the Stun Gun to eliminate him. However, a well-timed blow from brass knuckles and the referee missing Austin's foot on the rope resulted in Sandman becoming the new ECW World Heavyweight Champion.

STONE COLD GOES *YARD*

Having already guest-starred or cameoed multiple times on TV shows, Stone Cold Steve Austin tried his hand at movies. His motion picture debut was the 2005 remake of *The Longest Yard*, starring Adam Sandler and Chris Rock. Austin played the very unpleasant Guard Dunham, and aside from suffering a hamstring injury while running football training drills, he loved the movie-making experience. He particularly loved working with Sandler, and in 2013 the two reunited for the comedian's first movie sequel, *Grown Ups 2*.

RAW TITLE-BEARER

As of this writing, the WWE Championship has changed hands 15 times throughout the history of *Monday Night Raw*. Stone Cold Steve Austin has won the title on three of those occasions, against Kane, Undertaker, and Kurt Angle — more than any other WWE Superstar to date.

Austin also intervened in several matches on *Raw* to cause a WWE Title change, including the first-ever on WWE's flagship program. On February 17, 1997, The Texas Rattlesnake disrupted two attempts for WWE Champion Bret Hart and Sycho Sid to have a title bout, then blasted Hart with a steel chair to successfully cost the Hit Man his championship on the third try. He'd use the same weapon to unseat The Rock on January 4, 1999, and help a groggy Mankind pin the Corporate Champion in a historic *Raw* moment.

CROSS THIS STREET AT YOUR PERIL

In Lowell, MA, on September 1, 1998, Steve Austin became the first sports entertainer to have a street named after him. To commemorate WWE's inaugural *Raw* at the Tsongas Arena, city officials decided that for one day, the roadway leading to the then-new arena, John F. Cox Circle, would be renamed "Stone Cold Way." The then-WWE Champion wore a "New England Patriots 3:16" jersey to the special ceremony outside the Tsongas Arena, spoke alongside Lowell Mayor Eileen Donoghue, City Councilor Armand Mercier, and other dignitaries, and signed autographs for fans in attendance.

Just remember: If you're ever looking for the Tsongas Arena, don't put "Stone Cold Way" in the GPS. It was just a one-day deal.

FORK FEAR

What was it about vehicular vengeance and Stone Cold Steve Austin at the 1999 and 2000 editions of *Survivor Series*? Whereas he was on the receiving end in 1999, he was the driver one year later.

A No Disqualification Match at *Survivor Series* (November 19, 2000) gave Stone Cold the opportunity to deliver much-needed payback to Triple H, the man who orchestrated Rikishi's hit-and-run on Austin one year earlier. The Bionic Redneck got the better of a brutal in-ring exchange inside the Ice Palace in Tampa, FL, forcing a bloodied Triple H to retreat to the parking lot and wait inside his Lincoln Continental for the right time to strike. It never came. Using a SkyTrak forklift, Stone Cold trapped The Game in his vehicle, lifted the car more than 30 feet in the air, then let it flip over and crash down to the ground below.

The match was officially declared a No Contest, but it was pretty clear to everyone watching who won.

1:02

A VERY MINIMUM WAGE

Stone Cold Steve Austin earned every dime of his fame and fortune as a world-renowned WWE Superstar. On May 11, 1989, though, newbie Steve Williams earned $40 for his first match, against Frogman LeBlanc. When traveling on the road, he'd earn as little as $25 per match.

AUSTIN'S RISE AND *FALL BRAWL*

One can argue that *WCW Fall Brawl: War Games* (September 18, 1994) is the event that best represents the end of "Stunning" Steve Austin's rise in WCW. Austin had just taken possession of his second WCW United States Heavyweight Title after it was relinquished by an injured Ricky Steamboat. He had maybe five minutes, at best, to bask in the moment, as WCW Commissioner Nick Bockwinkel decreed that the new champion would not only still compete that night, but he had to defend the title as well. Out came his surprise challenger (and longtime Hulk Hogan associate) "Hacksaw" Jim Duggan, who squashed an incensed Austin in under a minute.

"Stunning" Steve would never see another championship for the remainder of his career in WCW.

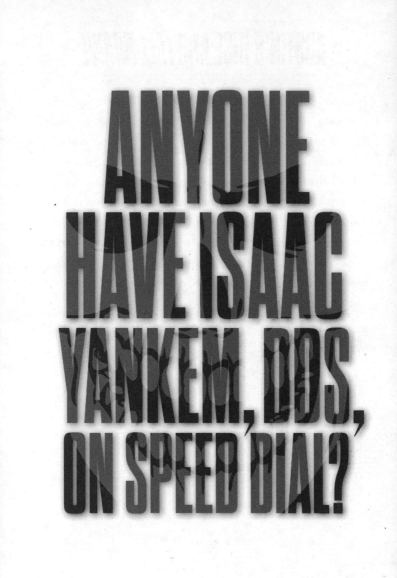

"From now on, it's open season on Vince McMahon. So, what that means is any time you show up at a *Monday Night Raw*, as soon as you step out of that car . . . Stone Cold Steve Austin can punch you right in the mouth. And the only thing you can do about it, Vince, is reach down, pick up your little teeth, put 'em in your shirt pocket, and go on about your business.

"If you decide not to come to work, that means Stone Cold can drive to Greenwich, CT, knock on your little front door. When you answer that front door, I can punch you right in your mouth. And the only thing you can do about it is pick up your little teeth, put 'em in your shirt pocket, and say, 'Linda! Stone Cold knocked out some more of my teeth!'"

In his final act as WWE CEO, Stone Cold Steve Austin puts himself back in the WWE Title hunt and serves notice to Mr. McMahon (*Raw*, June 28, 1999)

LEGEND OF THE FALL

Mr. Perfect: What happened to The Ringmaster?
Vince McMahon: I'm not certain. Must have been eliminated. We missed it.

The commentators at the 1996 edition of *Royal Rumble* weren't the only ones who missed it. As entrant No. 24, The Ringmaster was expected to be one of the final four Superstars in his first Royal Rumble Match. Just under 11 minutes later, though, he became the 23rd participant eliminated from the 30-man, over-the-top-rope contest. The No. 30 entrant — Duke "The Dumpster" Droese — hadn't even entered yet.

So, what happened? According to Stone Cold Steve Austin, he simply slipped over a portion of the top rope that had been made slick by some baby oil worn by Fatu. Adding insult to injury, Fatu was recorded as the Superstar who eliminated The Ringmaster.

CEMENTING HIS LEGACY

Mr. McMahon, broken leg and all, drove his prized, classic white Chevrolet Corvette C4 convertible into the backlot of the

Nassau Coliseum to attend *Raw* in Uniondale, NY, on October 12, 1998. By the end of the night, he required another means of transportation to leave the building.

From his private room, McMahon, Commissioner Slaughter, and corporate "stooges" Pat Patterson and Gerald Brisco watched on a monitor in horror as Stone Cold Steve Austin — still incensed after the WWE Chairman orchestrated his loss of the WWE Title at *Unforgiven: In Your House* — drove a cement mixer into the backlot. The Rattlesnake then lined up the mixer and proceeded to pour tons of cement into McMahon's Corvette. The vehicle's interior quickly filled with so much cement that the side windows shattered.

Stone Cold loved demolishing Mr. McMahon's ride that night, though he has admitted in numerous interviews that he would just as soon have taken the Corvette home as destroy it. WWE purchased the convertible from a salvage yard on the day of the "incident," and he thought it was in excellent condition. He also recalls learning how to drive and operate the controls inside the cement mixer approximately 20 minutes before the start of *Raw*.

Though the Corvette's fate was literally and figuratively "cemented" that night, it has since made some personal appearances, primarily at events such as WrestleMania Axxess. The vehicle currently resides within the WWE Archives Warehouse, and *man*, is it heavy.

BY AUSTIN BETRAYED

On July 22, 2001, at *InVasion*'s "Inaugural Brawl" (a Five-on-Five Tag Team Match), Stone Cold Steve Austin betrayed Mr. McMahon and Team WWE and defected to the WCW/ECW Coalition run by WCW owner Shane McMahon, ECW owner Stephanie McMahon, and ECW General Manager Paul Heyman. For the first time in sports-entertainment history, WCW and ECW had control of the WWE Championship that was held by Austin, plus the Hardcore Title won that night by Rob Van Dam.

A "HELL" OF A MATCH

Stone Cold Steve Austin took part in WWE's first and, to date, only Six-Man Hell in a Cell Match at *Armageddon* on December 10, 2000. Joining him in the unforgiving steel structure were The Rock, Undertaker, Rikishi, Triple H, and Kurt Angle, who was defending his WWE Championship in the match. A capacity crowd in Alabama's Birmingham-Jefferson Civic Center watched an unbelievably brutal confrontation that saw The Bionic Redneck nearly capture the WWE Title after hitting The Great One with a Stone Cold Stunner. However, The Game attacked

Austin before he could secure a three count, giving Angle ample time to weakly cover The Rock for the win.

AN ALLIANCE IS FORMED

After setting plans in motion with Rick Rude at *Halloween Havoc* and *Clash of the Champions XVII*, Paul E. Dangerously (Paul Heyman) introduced the world to his "Dangerous Alliance" on *WCW Saturday Night* (November 23, 1991) — a stable that consisted of new WCW United States Heavyweight Champion Rude, Arn Anderson, Larry Zbyszko, Madusa, "Beautiful" Bobby Eaton, and the man to whom Eaton had lost the WCW World Television Championship earlier that year, "Stunning" Steve Austin.

The potential of this incredibly formidable faction was never fully explored, though they made the most of their short time together. Austin considers his most memorable WCW event to be *Wrestle War '92*, headlined by the brutal, bloody WarGames Match between the Alliance and Sting's Squadron (Sting, Nikita Koloff, Dustin Rhodes, Ricky Steamboat, and Barry Windham).

Stone Cold: You think you're funny? Insulting me like that?

Crowd: *What?*

Stone Cold: Does it make you feel good?

Crowd: *What?*

Stone Cold: Does it?

Crowd: *What?*

Stone Cold: Does it make you feel more like a human being?

Crowd: *What?*

Stone Cold: Does it make you feel special?

Crowd: *What?*

Stone Cold: Does it make you feel proud?

Crowd: *What?* [*Crowd cheers.*]

Stone Cold: I can say right now, Rock . . . I've heard you talk about me before.

Crowd: *What?*

Stone Cold: Yeah, you said, "Yeah, Stone Cold Steve Austin, you come out there with your beer belly!"

Crowd: *What?*

Stone Cold: [*Motions to midsection.*] You called that a beer belly!

Crowd: *What?*

Stone Cold: You called that a *beer belly*!

Crowd: *What?*

Stone Cold: That ain't no beer belly. That's a fuel tank for a whoop-ass machine, and I'm about to *open up a can on your ass right now*!

Stone Cold and The Rock try to one-up each other one last time before *Survivor Series*'s Winner Take All match between The Alliance and Team WWE (*Raw*, November 12, 2001)

THE SCARIEST MOMENT OF AUSTIN'S LIFE

At the tenth annual *SummerSlam* (August 3, 1997), Stone Cold Steve Austin had to beat Intercontinental Champion Owen Hart for the title or kiss his ass. Late into the bout, a sit-down piledriver placed Austin's head about six inches below the bottom of Hart's legs, leaving him unprotected as his skull spiked downward into the canvas.

While going over their match earlier that night, Austin had expressed concern when Owen maintained that he'd do the piledriver in a sit-down position rather than from the knees. He assumed Hart could manage the move, but it didn't work out that way. Losing all feeling in his body from the neck down, Austin thought he had become paralyzed in a manner similar to actor Christopher Reeve.

Hart paraded around the ring and gloated to the capacity crowd, giving Austin time to recover enough and weakly roll him up from behind for the pinfall victory. It took the new Intercontinental Champion several long minutes before he could stand up and defiantly exit the ring under his own power.

Stone Cold has repeatedly asserted that he did not break his neck at *SummerSlam*; he suffered temporary paralysis and a severely bruised spinal cord. The injury would plague him and shorten his career, and its initial effects took Austin out of action for a few months. He had to forfeit his Intercontinental and World Tag Team Titles while WWE's creative adjusted storylines to keep him involved during his recovery.

AUSTIN'S SECOND WWE TITLE CHANGE

C ustomizing a title to befit a specific champion's persona has become more commonplace in WWE in recent years, but it wasn't always that way. Superstars like Ultimate Warrior and Billy Graham changed the color of their respective titles' leather straps, and a custom championship made in advance to fit Andre the Giant in 1987 was never worn (since he lost to Hulk Hogan at *WrestleMania III*). Otherwise, a title's look changed only with WWE's approval.

Of course, that changed with Stone Cold. On the July 27, 1998, edition of *Raw*, without WWE management's approval, Steve Austin headed to the ring carrying a brand-new WWE Championship that suited his hell-raisin' personality. Sporting a center plate that included rattlesnakes, barbed wire, and a human skull with gray smoke emanating from its eye sockets, Austin's self-commissioned "Smoking Skull" championship belt perfectly complemented its badass owner. Now more than ever, Austin personified WWE's Attitude Era.

ROGUE TO THE FINAL FOUR

B eing one of the last four remaining combatants in the 30-man, over-the-top-rope Royal Rumble Match is quite the accomplishment. Well, Stone Cold Steve Austin was the first WWE Superstar to do it *five times*. Furthermore, he won three of those contests, and he achieved all of this in a total of only six Royal Rumble Match appearances.

After his last Rumble in 2002 — which, subsequently, was his *final* final four appearance — Austin was in a league of his own for eight years. Since then, Shawn Michaels, Triple H, John Cena, and Roman Reigns have matched the Rattlesnake's five appearances, while Randy Orton and Kane have made it to the final four on six occasions. (For Kane, you have to count his one time as "Fake Diesel.")

1:14

TRACING THE HOLLYWOOD BLONDS' ROOTS

"**S**tunning" Steve Austin & "Flyin'" Brian Pillman weren't the first tag team to call themselves The Hollywood Blonds. In fact, they're actually one of *seven* tandems to use the moniker.

The original Blonds, Jerry Brown & Buddy Roberts, started up in 1970 and dominated the National Wrestling Alliance (NWA) Tri State, CWF, and NWA Hollywood Wrestling territories. Though Austin & Pillman are considered the most popular of the seven Blonds pairings, Brown & Roberts are the most decorated, winning 14 tag team titles before they disbanded in 1977.

Brown pursued a singles career in the south. Roberts, meanwhile, turned another tag team into an unforgettable three-man gang, joining Michael P.S. Hayes and Terry "Bam Bam" Gordy as part of the legendary Fabulous Freebirds.

1:15

WINNING WHEN IT MATTERS MOST

With his victories over Shawn Michaels and The Rock at *WrestleMania XIV* and *WrestleMania XV*, respectively, Stone Cold became the first of only three Superstars to win back-to-back World Titles at The Showcase of the Immortals. As of this writing, he remains the only Superstar to win the WWE Championship at consecutive *WrestleMania*s.

"Your little Hart Foundation that follows you around wherever you go is like a snake. . . . I know all about snakes, and if you want to kill a snake, the fastest way to kill the damn thing is to get your shovel and chop the head off! Bret Hart is the head of the snake, and if it would be the easiest thing for me to do, that's exactly what I'd do, because I can take Bret out with a snap of my fingers and everybody knows it! But what I'm gonna do, instead of being all business and goin' straight ahead, I'm gonna have a little fun with it, because this time, I ain't gonna chop the snake's head off and just end it like that. I'm gonna start with the snake's *ass*!

"And you ain't gotta look around with a questionable look on your face because if there is an ass to the snake machine of the Hart Foundation, the snake's ass is Brian Pillman! Brian Pillman, I crippled your sorry carcass once before, and for years and years in the bush leagues, I carried you right in my back pocket. But when the bell rings, and you look across the ring in the eyes of Stone Cold Steve Austin, you will know that your ass is mine! And that's the bottom line, 'cause Stone Cold said so!"

While being interviewed in the ring by Vince McMahon, The Texas Rattlesnake puts Bret Hart, Brian Pillman, and the Hart Foundation on notice (*Raw*, May 12, 1997)

WHAT A DIFFERENCE A YEAR MAKES

You could hardly call it a peaceful coexistence, but Stone Cold Steve Austin & Undertaker managed to stay on the same page long enough to defeat Mankind & Kane for the World Tag Team Titles at *Fully Loaded: In Your House*, on July 29, 1998.

One year later, though, it was a very different story. No longer tag team champions, The Texas Rattlesnake and the Corporate Ministry's Phenom again main-evented the *Fully Loaded* pay-per-view (July 25, 1999). However, this time they weren't on the same page, not on the same book . . . hell, not even in the same library. The only common interest they shared was to make the other see red in a WWE Championship First Blood Match that represented the "End of an Era" for either the champion Austin or the Corporate Ministry's "higher power," Mr. McMahon. Stone Cold remained golden after turning Undertaker's face into a crimson mask (though a post-match assault also left Austin a bloody mess), and the WWE Chairman was extremely blue as he was banished from ever appearing on WWE programing . . . at least for a few months.

AUSTIN DECONSTRUCTION

More than five months after having surgery on his C3 and C4 vertebrae, it was announced that Stone Cold Steve Austin would be in The Rock's corner for the WWE Championship Match at *Backlash* (April 30, 2000). Yet, in true Stone Cold fashion, he didn't wait that long to return to WWE.

On the final *SmackDown* before the pay-per-view, The Toughest S.O.B. in WWE appeared on the TitanTron, standing atop a large crane outside the parking lot of North Carolina's Charlotte Coliseum. The crane was positioned next to the McMahon-Helmsley regime's mobile base of operations, a tour bus called the DX Express.

Citing his penchant for destroying things, Stone Cold revealed the name on the side of the crane as "Austin Deconstruction," hopped into the vehicle, and dropped a large cement girder directly onto the DX Express. The crushed bus immediately blew up on impact, while Stephanie McMahon and Triple H watched from the ring in abject horror.

The DX Express reappeared again days later at *Backlash* . . . sort of. After helping The Rock defeat Triple H for the WWE Championship, Austin used his Stone Cold pickup truck to tow what was left of the bus into Washington, D.C.'s MCI Center.

A STUNNER FOR THE AGES

The oldest person ever to receive a Stone Cold Stunner is the late, great WWE Hall of Famer Mae Young. Young was 80 years old when she took a Stunner from The Texas Rattlesnake, who was competing against Eric Bischoff in a "Redneck Triathlon" at *Bad Blood* (June 15, 2003) to determine who was *Raw's* better Co-General Manager. Since he had already won the first leg of the triathlon, a Belching Contest, Austin opted to "forfeit" the second round to Bischoff, Stunning Young rather than engage with her in the stipulated "Pie-Eating Contest."

WHAT'S HIS POISON?

It's a question that has plagued and spurred debate within the WWE Universe for years: What beer did Stone Cold celebrate with inside the ring?

The Texas Rattlesnake says he rotated through many different brands, including Budweiser, Bud Light, Miller Light, and Busch Light. However, Mark Yeaton confirms that during his years as WWE's timekeeper, the go-to beverage he'd toss Austin was actually Natural Light.

STONE COLD ON ICE

Twenty-four hours after Undertaker and Kane simultaneously pinned Stone Cold Steve Austin at *Breakdown: In Your House*, Mr. McMahon prepared to present one of them with the WWE Championship on the September 28, 1998, edition of *Raw*. Despite having police protection on a red-carpeted ring inside Detroit's Joe Louis Arena, McMahon never got the chance. An enraged Stone Cold Steve Austin "borrowed" the Detroit Red Wings' ice-resurfacing Zamboni, drove it through locked gates and over light fixtures, and rammed it into the side of the ring. Austin then fired off a barrage of double birds and ran down the hood of the Miller Lite–adorned Zamboni, tackling McMahon with a flying clothesline.

The Texas Rattlesnake hissed and spewed venom as officers handcuffed and led him to a police car out back. "I ain't through with ya, Vince!" he yelled. "I ain't through with ya by a long shot!"

Fortunately, the Red Wings' NHL home opener wasn't for a few more weeks, so their fans didn't follow the tradition of throwing octopi onto the arena floor.

ANOTHER "STUNNING" TITLE RUN BEGINS

At WCW's annual extravaganza *Starrcade* (December 27, 1993), "Stunning" Steve Austin closed out 1993 on a high note, winning his first WCW United States Heavyweight Title by defeating fellow Texan "The Natural" Dustin Rhodes, in a physical Two Out of Three Falls Match. Austin claimed the first fall in controversial fashion after the official disqualified Rhodes, ruling he had thrown his opponent over the top rope. (A no-no in WCW at that time.)

Much of the second fall took place under limited lighting during an outage inside the Independence Arena in Charlotte, NC. Though it wasn't nearly as bad as the complete power outage Austin and Savio Vega would experience at WWE's *Beware of Dog* nearly three years later in *South* Carolina, the power surge may have momentarily thrown "The Natural" off his game. It didn't affect Austin; despite being busted open and receiving mounted punches in the corner, "Stunning" Steve pulled Rhodes down and rolled him up (with a handful of trunks) for the three count. Austin ended Rhodes's 119-day reign and began a 240-day run as WCW's United States Heavyweight Champion.

BRIDGE OVER TROUBLED WATER

S teve Austin was especially Stone Cold when *Raw* came to chilly Durham, NH, December 15, 1997. The Rock had demanded that Austin return his confiscated Intercontinental Title to the ring inside the Whittemore Center Arena. Suddenly, the TitanTron revealed the Rattlesnake was standing on the General Sullivan Bridge, a nine-span steel deck truss bridge that had been closed to vehicular traffic for more than a decade.

Austin reminded Rock that he had forfeited the title over to him one week earlier, but on this night, The Great One would have to make an effort to find it. The Toughest S.O.B. in WWE then took a mask, a snorkel, a regulator, an oxygen tank, flippers, a cell phone, a pager, and the Intercontinental Title, and proceeded to throw each of them over the bridge and into the frigid waters of the Piscataqua River below.

"Let him swim out there and find the damn thing," Austin said as he left the bridge. "If he's lucky, he'll find it. If he don't, maybe he'll drown. I really don't give a damn what he does."

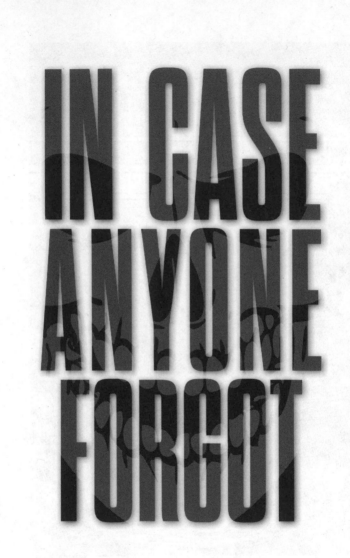

"You'll know that Stone Cold stands for two things:
It's 1) 'Don't Trust Anybody,' and 2) 'When in doubt, whoop
as much ass and raise as much hell as humanly possible.'"

Eric Bischoff is reminded as to who Stone
Cold really is during their *Survivor Series*
contract signing pitting Team Bischoff vs.
Team Austin (*Raw*, November 7, 2003)

THE GOLD STANDARD

As The Two-Man Power Trip, Stone Cold Steve Austin & Triple H are one of only five tandems in WWE history to simultaneously hold singles and tag team championships. The Texas Rattlesnake was WWE Champion and The Game held the Intercontinental Title when they defeated The Brothers of Destruction, Undertaker & Kane, for the World Tag Team Championship in a Winner Take All Match at *Backlash* (April 29, 2001).

The four other duos to wear singles and tag team gold include the "Two Dudes With Attitudes," Diesel (WWE Champion) & Shawn Michaels (Intercontinental Champion) (1995), Owen Hart (Intercontinental Champion) & British Bulldog (European Champion) (1997), Ken Shamrock (Intercontinental Champion) & Big Boss Man (Hardcore Champion) (1998), and Sasha Banks (Raw Women's Champion) & Bayley (SmackDown Women's Champion) (2020). With the exception of Banks & Bayley, all tandems held their individual titles *before* winning their tag team titles.

FIRST ROUND'S ON HIM

The March 22, 1999, *Raw* was truly an intoxicating moment in sports-entertainment history. With *WrestleMania XV* less than a week away, WWE Champion The Rock, Mr. McMahon, and Shane McMahon took to the ring inside Albany, NY's Pepsi Arena to smack-talk Stone Cold Steve Austin and continue stacking the decks in their favor. Suddenly, Stone Cold's music hit, and The Texas Rattlesnake headed to the ring . . . driving a 16-foot Coors Light beer truck!

The capacity crowd erupted as Austin pulled up to the ring, faced down his enemies and, faster than a silver bullet, fired off a high-pressure water hose filled with the good stuff. The McMahons and The Great One were drenched and practically drowning in beer, while the audience in attendance and watching from home drank in every moment of a historic confrontation that had everyone buzzed — sorry, *buzzing*.

1:27

SATURDAY NIGHT'S ALL RIGHT FOR FIGHTING

With the exception of The Rock, Stone Cold battled every member of Mr. McMahon's Corporation in a Corporate Gauntlet Match on *Raw* February 13, 1999. Before 41,432 WWE Universe members inside Toronto's SkyDome — an attendance record for *Raw* that remains to this day — Steve Austin nearly ran the "McMahondated" gauntlet, withstanding attacks from Ken Shamrock, Test, Kane, and Chyna that earned each of them a disqualification. Unfortunately, a nightstick beatdown from Big Boss Man allowed the match's final participant, Mr. McMahon, to cover the fallen Rattlesnake.

Broadcast 24 hours before Austin and McMahon's Steel Cage Match at *St. Valentine's Day Massacre: In Your House*, this edition of *Raw* aired on a Saturday. The event took place on February 8, but the show was pre-empted from its Monday night slot due to the Westminster Kennel Club Dog Show. Man, that's *ruff*.

CHAMPION BY NUMBERS

Combined, Stone Cold Steve Austin's six WWE Championship reigns total more than 17 months. Here's how they break down:

- March 29–June 28, 1998: 91 days
- June 29–September 27, 1998: 90 days
- March 28–May 23, 1999: 56 days
- June 28–August 22, 1999: 55 days
- April 1–September 23, 2001: 175 days
- October 8–December 9, 2001: 62 days

At 529 days, The Texas Rattlesnake has the tenth longest combined reign of all WWE Champions. Even his shortest run with the title (55 days) is longer than six of The Rock's eight WWE

Championships. Of the nine Superstars ahead of Austin, only two are fully active today: Brock Lesnar and Randy Orton.

1:29

HART'S ORIGINAL
WRESTLEMANIA 13 OPPONENT

S tone Cold Steve Austin and Bret Hart's Submission Match at *WrestleMania 13* is a seminal moment in WWE history that almost didn't happen. The Hit Man's victory over Austin at *Survivor Series* in November 1996 was supposed to pull back on their rivalry and begin a push toward Hart vs. Michaels II, with HBK defending the WWE Title this time. In February 1997, however, Michaels relinquished the championship due to a serious knee injury. It was then determined that the WWE Title picture would focus on Sycho Sid and Undertaker, while Austin and Hart would resume their conflict heading into The Showcase of the Immortals — a conflict that both Superstars initially thought was happening too soon.

WERE THEY MADE OF SNAKESKIN?

B ack in the late '90s, Stone Cold merchandise was *everywhere* — T-shirts, baseball caps, action figures . . . and more than a few novelty items pitched went beyond the norm of sports entertainment.

Case in point: LifeStyles Condoms' proposed "Austin 3:16" sheath. The condom may have been made with the intent of raising hell, but the copy on its packaging encouraged its wearer to "Play Safe." The packaging also included WWE's Attitude scratch logo, the Austin catchphrase "Gimme a Hell Yeah!", directions on how to use the prophylactic, and Stone Cold's vital statistics (naturally).

According to an episode of Bruce Prichard's podcast series *Something to Wrestle With* . . . , there was a pitch to WWE for a series of Superstar-themed condoms. He doesn't believe the deal ever came to fruition, though one can find the occasional "Austin 3:16" condom for sale online. (Unopened, we hope.)

WHO IS THAT MASKED CHAMPION?

S tone Cold Steve Austin was on the losing side of history when he and Kane battled in a First Blood Match for the WWE Championship at *King of the Ring* (June 28, 1998). Though

Kane's title reign was only 24 hours long, his victory made The Big Red Machine the first masked Superstar ever to win WWE's ultimate prize.

1:32

TAKING A LEAP FORWARD

On May 11, 1989, those attending the Dallas Sportatorium for WCCW action witnessed a very inexperienced Steve Austin — or Williams, rather — make his debut against Frogman LeBlanc, a journeyman Cajun grappler whose list of opponents would include Bobby Eaton, Dustin Rhodes, Jeff Jarrett, Cactus Jack, and Sting. The match was disastrous in the future Stone Cold's eyes. Though his mentor "Gentleman" Chris Adams had taught him some in-ring maneuvers, Adams never explained things like kayfabe, how to safely "work" an opponent, or utilize ring psychology. The result was a match filled with stiff arm-drags and armbars, and referee Tony Falk calling moves to help Williams get through the bout and pick up the victory.

The match result was the same when the two met again on *USWA Championship Sports* April 21, 1990. This time, however, LeBlanc found himself up against a far more polished, knowledgeable opponent in "Stunning" Steve Austin.

AUSTIN'S "SHERIFFMOBILE"

"The way I got it figured, I'm guessing you got
about a 15-, 20-yard head start. If I was you, I'd turn
around and haul ass!" — **Stone Cold Steve Austin**

Never antagonize a Rattlesnake, especially one that's in posses-
sion of a Stone Cold–themed Polaris 700cc four-wheel ATV.
Mr. McMahon thought otherwise when he chose to lambast
Raw's Sheriff, Stone Cold Steve Austin, from atop the ramp of
Atlanta, GA's Gwinnett Center on March 1, 2004. It earned the
Chairman an extremely uncomfortable up-close look at Austin's
"Redneck Special," which nearly ran him down backstage until
McMahon escaped into his limousine. That didn't stop The
Texas Rattlesnake, who drove the ATV directly onto the top of
the limo. He then revved up the engine until the ATV's exhaust
fumes seeped into the limo's open sunroof. McMahon barely
managed to get to the driver's side of the limo and sped off, with
Austin chasing him down the streets of Atlanta.

1:34

"One of these days, I'm gonna look down at your grave and it's gonna say, 'Here lies Bret "The Hit Man" Hart, the biggest piece of crap that ever walked the face of the Earth. And the reason he's lying here is because *Steve Austin whipped his pink-and-black ass*!' And that's the bottom line, 'cause Stone Cold said so!"

Stone Cold responds after Bret Hart says he's done with The Texas Rattlesnake following their *WrestleMania 13* Submission Match (*Raw*, March 31, 1997)

FOLEY'S FIRST IMPRESSION OF AUSTIN

While running around WCCW as Cactus Jack Manson in 1989, Mick Foley sat high inside the Dallas Sportatorium one night and watched "Gentleman" Chris Adams teach his wrestling class to the young hopefuls that had signed up. None of the students impressed him except for a tall, blond-haired guy with an athletic build named Steve Williams. Watching how Williams conducted himself in the class, Foley thought he was okay; in fact, he was quite sure Williams would make a name for himself. Twenty-seven years later, the WWE Hall of Famer shared his story with Steve Austin and the WWE Universe in Arlington, TX, during a WrestleMania Axxess edition of *Stone Cold Podcast*.

TIME KEEPER

Stone Cold kept checking an imaginary watch while waiting for opponents to enter the 1997 Royal Rumble Match, but Steve Austin's lifelong affinity for timepieces is genuine. Admittedly obsessed with time and a stickler for punctuality, Austin's vast collection includes the likes of Omega, Citizen, IWC, Rolex, Panerai, Sinn, Luminox, Breitling, and Kobold. It cannot be confirmed if all of his watches are set to 3:16.

STEVEAMANIA RUNS WILD IN ECW

Shortly after his unceremonious release from WCW, Steve Austin made a stunning appearance when he interrupted announcer Joey Styles at the end of *ECW Hardcore TV* on September 26, 1995. Austin spoke and dressed like a very poor man's Hulk Hogan, complete with yellow "Steveamania Rules" T-shirt and bandana. What he had to say, though, stands out as an extreme example of his incredible mic skills and on-camera presence.

Joey Styles: You're Steve Austin!

Austin: Y'know, that's where you're wrong, Mean Joey! Because Steve Austin doesn't have what it takes to get it done in the ECW, brother! I was never allowed to reach past mid-card status in the WCW, brother! So you know what, dude? I looked at the greatest Heavyweight Champions of all time, brother, and I knew — I *knew* — that I had to say my prayers! I had to take the vitamins! Brother, I had to start trainin' again! I had to get my mind right to do what it takes to get it done in the ECW, dude! And let me tell ya something — I've been —

Johnny Grunge: Steveamania! Ohhhh! I'm a Steveamaniac . . . !

Austin: Let me tell ya somethin', dude: The Stevester's here! Steveamania's gonna run wild on the ECW, brother! Steveamania! I'm takin' the vitamins! I'm sayin' my prayers! I . . . [*Removes bandana, tears off "Steveamania" shirt.*] I'm not gonna do this sh*t anywhere! Not even in ECW! Because there's no way this lame-ass sh*t is gonna get the job done *anywhere*!

A LINCOLN MEMORIAL

The Rock intended the April 19, 1999, edition of *Raw* to be a funeral for the career of Stone Cold Steve Austin. Instead, the evening turned out to be the figurative assassination of a Lincoln Continental.

A week after hurling Austin off a bridge and into the Detroit River, The Rock prepared a service and eulogy within the Van Andel Arena in Grand Rapids, MI, complete with a hearse, a casket, flowers, and a large mound of dirt. Before he could pay his final disrespects, however, the TitanTron showed Stone Cold's Austin 3:16 monster truck arriving outside the arena's parking lot, where The Great One had parked his brand-new $40,000 Lincoln Continental. After circling the vehicle a few times, Austin drove the monster truck right on top of the Lincoln, crushing it beyond recognition. R.I.P., Lincoln Continental.

DRAFT DODGER

All WWE Superstars were eligible for the inaugural WWE Draft that commenced on *Raw* and on WWE.com April 1, 2002. Though WWE's Undisputed Champion and the WWE Women's

Champion could compete on both *Raw* and *SmackDown*, no one Superstar was exempt . . . except for Stone Cold Steve Austin.

WWE's then-CEO, Linda McMahon, declared The Texas Rattlesnake a free agent, meaning he could sign with either Ric Flair, who controlled *Raw*, or Vince McMahon, who controlled *SmackDown*. When Austin came down to the ring to address both men, he said he'd sign with the blue brand . . . then followed up with an "April Fool's" and Stunnered McMahon. A jubilant Flair styled and profiled to celebrate Austin signing with *Raw*, only to eat a Stone Cold Stunner as well. Stone Cold signed the *Raw* contract, but he made it clear to everyone that he was no one's property.

1:40

FROM VIVACIOUS TO BLOSSOMING

When "Stunning" Steve Austin made his World Championship Wrestling debut on *WCW Saturday Night* (May 25, 1991), he was accompanied to the ring by a brash, blond valet named "Vivacious Veronica." She was a trained wrestler and the real-life girlfriend of Rex King, whom the WWE Universe would recognize as Timothy Well, one half of the tag team Well Dunn.

After an initial series of WCW tapings, it was decided there wasn't much chemistry between Veronica and Austin, so she was removed without explanation. "Stunning" Steve was quickly paired up with Lady Blossom, aka Jeanie Clarke, Austin's girlfriend and valet from WCCW/USWA.

A SUBMISSION MATCH? REALLY?

Initially, both Stone Cold Steve Austin and Bret Hart thought it was too soon to face off again at *WrestleMania 13*, only four months after their memorable clash at *Survivor Series*. Both were particularly unhappy about it being announced as a Submission Match, a stipulation Austin only found out about while rehabbing his left knee on his couch in San Antonio, TX. As he recalled with the Hit Man on *Steve Austin's Broken Skull Sessions*, "I was like, *What the f*ck? I'm not even a submission wrestler! I don't even know any holds!* I was mad as a hornet."

Thankfully, it worked out pretty well at The Show of Shows, even becoming one of Stone Cold's two all-time favorite matches.

1:42

"I think we got another T-shirt on the way, and
I think that T-shirt might just say, 'McMahon
3:16 says, "I just pissed my pants!"'"

Stone Cold comments on Mr. McMahon's in-ring
accident after firing off a toy gun with a scroll that
pops out saying "Bang 3:16" (*Raw*, October 19, 1998)

RAW'S HIGHEST RATED EPISODE

The blockbuster main event of Stone Cold Steve Austin, The Rock, & Vince McMahon vs. Triple H, Undertaker, & Shane McMahon — officiated by Shawn Michaels, no less — is responsible for the most viewed episode in *Raw*'s history. The show, which emanated from Florida's Orlando Arena on May 10, 1999, averaged an unbelievable 8.1 rating and a 12.1 share, reaching 6.148 million homes and 9.2 million viewers. Simply stated, approximately one out of every 12 televisions with cable showed that evening's *Raw*, which saw Stone Cold hit Shane-O-Mac with a Stone Cold Stunner, pull Mr. McMahon off his attempted pinfall of Shane, then Stunner Shane again to collect the three count himself.

How did *WCW Monday Nitro* fare that evening? It didn't. TNT pre-empted the show in favor of the NBA Playoffs. The Portland Trail Blazers beat the Phoenix Suns that night, 110–99, in case you're interested.

"MONEY" TALKS

As The Ringmaster, Steve Austin had two entrance themes. The second was titled, appropriately enough, "Ringmaster." However, the first theme he came out to was actually "It's All About the Money," which belonged to The Million Dollar Man, Ted DiBiase.

1:45

MAKING A GREAT FIRST IMPRESSION

It took more than seven years for Steve Austin to become sports entertainment's biggest star, but *Pro Wrestling Illustrated* (*PWI*) recognized his greatness right away. Austin won the *PWI* 1990 Rookie of the Year Award, with El Gigante, Brad Anderson, and Chris Chavis placing as the first, second, and third runners-up, respectively. The award has also gone to notable ring legends including Ric Flair, Ricky Steamboat, Madusa Miceli (aka Alundra Blayze), Lex Luger, Owen Hart, Goldberg, and Kurt Angle, as well as legends in the making such as Randy Orton, Bobby Lashley, Charlotte Flair, Nia Jax, Otis, and Ronda Rousey.

1:46

SO NICE HE DID IT TWICE

In winning the World Tag Team, Intercontinental, and WWE Championships within a two-year span, Stone Cold Steve Austin became WWE's fifth Triple Crown Champion, preceded only by Pedro Morales, Bret Hart, Diesel, and Shawn Michaels.

Even more impressive is the fact that he won each of those titles *twice* in that same two-year span, making him the third-ever, two-time Triple Crown Champion in WWE history. The previous Superstars to accomplish that feat are the Hit Man and the Showstopper that Austin defeated for the WWE Title.

1:47

BEDPAN LINER NOTES

Like most fans, Steve Austin has very fond memories of the "Bedpan McMahon" incident in October 1998, albeit for different reasons. First, while Mr. McMahon was tended to in his hospital bed, Stone Cold and Mankind went over their respective plans for the Chairman inside the room's bathroom — laughing so loudly that the TV crew had to repeatedly ask them to quiet down while they shot footage. As for using a bedpan on McMahon's skull, the Rattlesnake credits the Chairman for that idea. Austin expressed genuine concern about blasting him with the five-pound, stainless steel object. Mr. McMahon insisted, however, so Stone Cold obliged.

1:48

HEY, THAT GUY LOOKS LIKE STONE COLD

In addition to siblings Kevin, Scott, Jeff, and Jennifer, Steve Austin has a half-brother whose on-screen work, bald head, and goatee has resulted in people mistaking him for Stone Cold. Jamie McBride, a veteran police officer and director of the Los Angeles Police Protective League, is also an actor who's appeared in such films as Michael Mann's *Collateral* and Michael Bay's *The Island* and *Transformers*. The lead characters in the 2012 film *End of Watch*, starring Jake Gyllenhaal and Michael Peña, are loosely based on McBride and fellow LAPD officer Charles Wunder.

1:49

THREE STAGES OF HELL? YEAH!

To settle their way-out-of-control rivalry, Mr. McMahon decreed that at *No Way Out* (February 25, 2001), Stone Cold Steve Austin and Triple H would meet in a best-of-three contest that became the first-ever Three Stages of Hell Match. The first match was a traditional singles bout, which Austin won with a Stunner, while the second fall, a Street Fight, went to the sledgehammer-wielding Cerebral Assassin. Their rubber match inside a steel cage was a brutal, bloody affair that witnessed The Game hit Austin with the sledgehammer just as the Rattlesnake struck Triple H with a 2 x 4 wrapped in barbed wire. Both kayoed Superstars fell to the canvas, but Triple H landed on top of Austin for the win.

Perhaps they knocked some sense into each other that night; just over a month later, Austin and Triple H joined forces to become The Two-Man Power Trip.

A REGAL ENDING TO THEIR REIGN

The Hollywood Blonds' 168-day WCW/NWA World Tag Team Title reign came to an end at *WCW Clash of the Champions XXIV*, at the hands of Four Horsemen members "The Enforcer" Arn Anderson & "Pretty" Paul Roma. Oddly enough, however, it wasn't "Stunning" Steve Austin & "Flyin'" Brian Pillman who lost the titles. Lord Steven Regal (whom the WWE Universe knows as William Regal) was made an honorary Blond to substitute for the injured Pillman. Despite their protests of conspiracy, the makeshift Blonds battled fiercely until Anderson knocked Austin into Regal's manager, Sir William (aka Bill Dundee). He then rolled up "Stunning" Steve for the victory and title change.

THE RATTLESNAKE'S ALL ABOUT "NATURE"

Though Steve Austin has great respect for many ring legends, he has gone on the record as saying that his all-time favorite sports entertainer is Ric Flair, and that he emulated his ring style after the Nature Boy. Whether you like it or you don't like it, learn to love it. And that's the bottom line, 'cause Stone Cold said so! *Woooooo!*

1:52

"I appreciate the fact you had to whip somebody's
ass, you had to kick somebody's ass, not *lick*
it, to get a goddamn championship belt!"

"The Extreme Superstar" Steve Austin confronts ECW
World Heavyweight Champion The Sandman at the
Sportland Café in Middletown, NY (September 23, 1995)

SLEEP ON IT

Before Stone Cold started dishing out the Stone Cold Stunner in WWE, Steve Austin put opponents to sleep with The Million Dollar Man's finisher, the Million Dollar Dream. Austin admits that he and the fans thought he was already doing that with his Ringmaster gimmick.

YOU'RE THINKING OF THE ICE CREAM

WWE was the hottest ticket in entertainment when Vince McMahon announced "Iron" Mike Tyson's involvement at *WrestleMania XIV*, and Stone Cold promptly disrupted the announcement with a verbal and double-middle-fingered barrage at The Baddest Man on the Planet. In reality, Austin and Tyson enjoyed working with each other . . . even though "Iron" Mike had trouble remembering Stone Cold's moniker.

Beginning with the moment he mentioned The Rattlesnake's name in an interview before the 1998 Royal Rumble Match, and in appearances all the way up to The Showcase of the Immortals, Tyson sometimes referred to Austin as "Cold Stone." Despite being a huge WWE fan, he just couldn't get the name right. The Scottsdale, AZ–based creamery chain must have loved that free business.

A MOUNT RUSHMORE LIKE NO OTHER

During a June 2020 interview with ComicBook.com, Undertaker revealed the ring legends he would choose to have immortalized on his "Mount Rushmore of Wrestling." Basing his choices on what each legend contributed to sports entertainment, The Phenom replied with the incredible list of Ric Flair, Hulk Hogan, Andre the Giant, and Stone Cold Steve Austin.

1:56

STEVE AUSTIN TEAMS WITH STEVE WILLIAMS

For one night only, Steve Austin partnered with the man who shared the same real name as he. "Dr. Death" Steve Williams was in need of a tag team partner when Terry "Bam Bam" Gordy didn't show up for WCW's *Halloween Havoc* (October 25, 1992). "Stunning" Steve was recruited to fly to Philadelphia right away and compete at the pay-per-view.

Despite having never worked in tandem before, the team of "Steve Williams" & Steve Williams battled Unified World Tag Team Champions Dustin Rhodes & Barry Windham to a

30-minute draw that night. Though they didn't partner again, "Dr. Death" would join WWE for a brief time in May 1998, when the champion was Stone Cold Steve *Austin*.

1:57

THE MOST IMPORTANT MATCH AUSTIN EVER LOST — *TWICE*

B ad weather and losing a Caribbean Strap Match to Savio Vega at *In Your House: Beware of Dog* was pivotal for Stone Cold Steve Austin. First, when Austin's Ringmaster persona lost the match to Vega at the pay-per-view on May 26, 1996, no one outside South Carolina's Florence Civic Center saw it. A severe local thunderstorm had cut off power at the arena and on WWE's pay-per-view feed, resulting in most of the event's matches not making it to broadcast.

When the following night's *Raw* announced *Beware of Dog 2* for May 28, a stipulation was added to the Caribbean Strap Match: The Ringmaster's manager, Ted DiBiase, declared he would leave WWE if his Million Dollar Champion lost the contest. It turned out that DiBiase had given notice after the first *Beware of Dog*, so the do-over allowed for WWE to build his departure into the storyline. Upon losing the match a second time, Austin had effectively won his freedom from the Ringmaster character he disliked, and he could start speaking for himself now that he no longer had a manager. (He also stopped carrying the Million Dollar Championship after that night.)

As for the second reason why the loss was key to Stone Cold's career, Bruce Prichard explained on an episode of his podcast *Something to Wrestle With . . .* that Vince McMahon was impressed by Austin's ring performance during the power outage. It had convinced him that Austin was the right choice to win the upcoming King of the Ring Tournament.

1:58

DESTINED TO FIGHT

It seems like Stone Cold Steve Austin's path was preordained to cross with The Rock's — before facing Shawn Michaels for the WWE Championship at *WrestleMania XIV*, The Texas Rattlesnake's last match on *Raw* was against his *WrestleMania XV* opponent, The Rock. At this point, The Great One was still Intercontinental Champion, three and a half months after Austin had forfeited it to him. The two would clash one-on-one on *Raw* only one more time before they met for the WWE Title at *WrestleMania XV*.

ON THE CLOCK

While growing up in Edna, TX, Steve Austin acquired his mother's interest in antique collecting. His interest manifested mainly in antique porcelain enamel signs related to Coca-Cola, gas, and oil, as well as other Coca-Cola memorabilia.

After being fired from WCW and moving back to Texas, Austin also developed a fascination with collecting neon clocks, particularly those promoting classic beer brands. He became so enamored with them, in fact, that he decided to learn how to build them. He devoted an episode of *The Steve Austin Show* to the art of neon clock collecting and bending neon tubes. If you look on Austin's Instagram or Twitter accounts (@steveaustinbsr), you'll see the occasional photo of his collection, located mostly within his bar setup at Broken Skull Ranch.

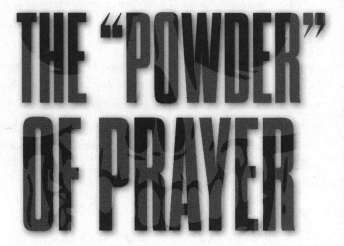

THE "POWDER"
OF PRAYER

"I don't know where the hell you're goin',
but you better give yourself to the Lord or
somebody, because your ass is mine!"

The Toughest S.O.B. in WWE interrupts Brian
Pillman, Owen Hart, and British Bulldog's in-ring
prayer session and chases them out into the
crowd with an ax handle (*Raw*, April 28, 1997)

A *GOOD PLACE* FOR STONE COLD

On the acclaimed television sitcom *The Good Place* (2016–2020), The Bionic Redneck is a recurring reference and a monster crush for Eleanor Shellstrop, played by Kristen Bell. "I've only said 'I love you' to two people in my life," she said in the season 2 episode "Dance Dance Resolution." "Stone Cold Steve Austin, and a guy in a dark club who I mistook for Stone Cold Steve Austin."

The series' penultimate episode, "Patty," puts the show's protagonists at a post-afterlife party that's tailored to everyone's individual desires. That includes Eleanor, who quickly discovers how her essence is being represented: Through the bedpan Stone Cold used to whack Mr. McMahon's skull in 1998.

In September 2019, The Texas Rattlesnake responded to Eleanor on a video online, stating, "You have great taste and, I must add, you are a legit snack."

AUSTIN & MICK FOLEY'S TAG TEAM HISTORY BEFORE WWE

Stone Cold didn't want to pair up and win WWE's World Tag Team Titles with Dude Love (Mick Foley) in 1997. However,

"Stunning" Steve Austin had no issue partnering with Cactus Jack (also Foley) in World Championship Wrestling. Their first pairing took place at a WCW event in Kansas City, MO's Municipal Auditorium on May 9, 1992, where they defeated Ron Simmons & Junkyard Dog. Though they'd compete together and against each other in WCW tag competition on several occasions, no iterations of Austin or Foley would battle one-on-one until *Raw* came to Connecticut's New Haven Coliseum on November 18, 1996. Stone Cold picked up the victory over Mankind in a No Holds Barred Match, thanks to interference from the masked Executioner (aka Terry Gordy).

1:03

STONE COLD VS. STING? ALMOST

In Jon Robinson's *WWE: The Attitude Era*, Sting revealed that he almost signed a deal with WWE in 2003 that would have him debut at the end of *WrestleMania XIX* and start a rivalry with Stone Cold Steve Austin. The Texas Rattlesnake later admitted that he had no idea about a possible buildup to Austin vs. Sting, and the point soon became moot, anyway; negotiations with the Stinger fell through, while Austin wrestled The Rock in what would be Stone Cold's final match.

A NAME YOU CAN DANCE TO?

Interested in sports entertainment from a young age, the future Stone Cold Steve Austin told his brothers that his ring name would be "The Western Fandango, Steve Williams."

Obviously, the name didn't stick.

A STONE COLD DAY IN HELL?

The temperature outside Virginia's Richmond Coliseum hovered around the low to mid-60s on May 11, 1997. Inside the arena, however, it was *A Cold Day in Hell*, WWE's latest installment of its *In Your House* events. Stone Cold Steve Austin faced WWE Champion Undertaker in what was the Rattlesnake's first one-on-one pay-per-view opportunity for the title. Late in the match, Austin connected with a Stone Cold Stunner that looked like it might give him the victory. Unfortunately, the ring bell rang prematurely, causing a distraction long enough for The Phenom to rally and get the win.

It wasn't the timekeeper who rang the bell, however. It was Brian Pillman, Austin's former Hollywood Blonds partner from WCW, who had aligned himself with The Hart Foundation. The Rattlesnake wouldn't see another WWE Title opportunity until March 1998 at *WrestleMania XIV*.

"Hello, everybody, and welcome to 'Monday NyQuil,' where the big boys play with each other! I apologize for the balloons, but I had to fire the pyro technician guy because he couldn't show up! I did it over the phone, no less, but I *had* to fire him!

"Okay, right here, where the big boys play with each other, on my right as of always, Bongo! [*Turns to a set of bongos representing Steve "Mongo" McMichael.*] Bongo, how you doin'? Okay! [*Knocks bongos off the table.*] The Brain couldn't be here tonight! Pan over here to where The Brain's supposed to be! Brain couldn't be here, so I had my secretary leave a message on his answering machine, and when he calls me, I'm gonna fire him on the phone just like I did Austin, because that's the way I deal with people! I'm not a very brave man, and *that's the bottom line*!

"Okay, big show tonight! Like I said, if you're watchin' another channel, get over here! If you're thinkin' of watchin' another wrestling promotion, don't do it, because this is the only one that's live! Okay, big main event tonight, never before seen on TV, the most dangerous match in the world, and you're gonna see it right here on 'Monday NyQuil!' Oh yeah, yes, right here on 'Monday NyQuil': *Bottle of Geritol on a Pole Match*! First time ever in the world! You're gonna see all the old codgers here in our organization, and they're gonna be scrappin' around and usin' their walkers, tryin' to keep their dentures in, and they're *goin'* for it, because this is the hottest show on TV! Brother, *this is the bottom line!*

"We're number one! And I repeat that I already fired The Brain over the phone! Oh yeah, this is where the big boys play with each other! Oh yeah, did I tell you that we're number one? Okay, I'm gonna . . . okay, the cameraman's tellin' me we gotta go to a break! I'm gonna tell you right now, I don't know the names of any of the holds, but I'm gonna sit here and fumble around and bumble around, and . . . if I *don't* put you to sleep, the matches probably will! So bear with us! This is 'Monday NyQuil,' and *we're live*!"

"The Extreme Superstar" Steve Austin satirizes his former employer Eric Bischoff to present "Monday NyQuil" and open *ECW Hardcore TV* (October 31, 1995)

"AUSTIN 3:16"? I DON'T GET IT

After Stone Cold Steve Austin won the 1996 King of the Ring Tournament and gave his "Austin 3:16" speech, he suggested that WWE make a plain black T-shirt with just "Austin 3:16" in white lettering on the front. According to Bruce Prichard's podcast *Something to Wrestle With . . .* WWE Chairman Vince McMahon wasn't so sure on the concept. He was concerned the WWE Universe wouldn't get it and might prefer a design that more visibly showed their support of Austin. Furthermore, WWE execs had been initially thinking about producing Austin's merchandise around the catchphrase "'Cause Stone Cold said so."

Everyone's thinking changed at *Raw* the following night (June 24, 1996). The Brown County Expo in Green Bay, WI, was littered with handmade fan signs that said "Austin 3:16." Don't let it be said that the Chairman and WWE don't listen to their fans.

LAND OF THE RISING STUN

"Stunning" Steve Austin made his Japan debut on August 6, 1992, when he appeared alongside several other WCW stars for New Japan Pro-Wrestling's G1 (Grade One) Climax tournament. This competition was held as a 16-man, single-elimination tournament for the vacant NWA World Heavyweight Title, and Austin's first-round opponent was his Dangerous Alliance cohort, Arn Anderson. Neither man knew they were facing each other until they arrived in Japan, following a long flight with a significant amount of beer drinking. The duo managed to put on a thrilling match, regardless, with the Stun Gun giving Austin the victory. He'd fall in the quarterfinals to Keiji Mutoh.

1:69

JAKE GETS SNAKED AGAIN

Jake "The Snake" Roberts competed in his final WWE pay-per-view as an entrant in the 1997 Royal Rumble Match. He was eliminated in just over a minute by the serpentine Superstar who beat him in the King of the Ring finals seven months earlier, Stone Cold Steve Austin.

1:70

IS IT ANY WONDER WHY HE DEFECTED?

Stone Cold lost four of his six WWE Championships to the Team WWE members he partnered with at the *InVasion* pay-per-view (July 22, 2001) — Kane (1988), Undertaker (1999), Kurt Angle (2001), and Chris Jericho (2001).

IT'S HIS BIG BREAK

It appears that even Steve Austin's friends aren't exempt from The Texas Rattlesnake's bite.

Paul Lazenby was Stone Cold's stunt double for six movies, including *The Package*, *Maximum Conviction*, *Tactical Force*, *Recoil*, *Hunt to Kill*, and *The Stranger*. In the first movie they worked together, the 2009 underground fighting movie *Damage*, Lazenby played Austin's opponent. And in one scene, Austin accidentally broke Lazenby's nose.

The good-natured Lazenby called the accident a career highlight, and he and Austin laughed it off. However, it was probably a wise move on his part just to be Stone Cold's stunt double afterward.

I'LL DRINK TO THAT

After so many years downing Steveweisers inside a WWE ring, Steve Austin took to making his own craft beer. Though a light beer drinker for most of his adult life, he took a shine to craft beers a year or two before he met Rob Croxall, proprietor and brewer of Los Angeles–based El Segundo Brewing Company (ESBC). Croxall would churn out a recipe that appealed to the WWE Hall of Famer's palette, and on November 13, 2015, Austin and ESBC launched Steve Austin's Broken Skull IPA.

A 6.7% alcohol by volume beverage "designed for the working man and woman," and featuring Citra, Cascade, and Chinook hops, Steve Austin's Broken Skull IPA was originally accessible only on the West Coast. Today, the beverage is now available throughout most locations across the United States, and growing.

CAN HE TALK?

Right after "Stunning" Steve Austin was fired by WCW in 1995, he received a call from his former Dangerous Alliance manager, Paul Heyman, who was running Extreme Championship Wrestling. Heyman invited him to come to ECW, and when Austin explained he was still rehabbing his arm injury, he replied, "Can you talk?" Surprised that Heyman was willing to pay him once a week to travel to Philadelphia and cut promos, Austin accepted.

When Austin arrived for his first taping, the Extreme front-runner told him to talk about anything he wanted, including how he felt about WCW and being fired. Having such an open platform inspired Austin to cut a series of promos and vent about the years of frustration he felt at WCW. It showcased his tremendous mic skills and ability to improvise, and other promotions, including WWE, quickly took notice. Austin credits Heyman for giving him that platform and feedback on what he was saying without telling him how to say it.

A STONE COLD CHRISTMAS

WWE's inaugural *Tribute to the Troops* was a December 25, 2003, edition of *SmackDown* entitled "Christmas from Baghdad." Recorded five days earlier from Fort Victory in Baghdad, Iraq — only one week after U.S. armed forces captured Saddam Hussein — the special event even featured Santa Claus, who handed out presents to the troops in attendance. Mr. McMahon, annoyed that he didn't get a gift, badmouthed and sucker-punched Jolly Ol' St. Nick, who then revealed himself as Stone Cold Steve Austin. He didn't bring a Christmas turkey, but Austin did offer up two middle-fingered birds before dropping the Chairman with a Stone Cold Stunner.

Later, after John Cena toppled Big Show with an Attitude Adjustment in the main event, Stone Cold Claus gifted the wise-cracking Dr. of Thuganomics a Stunner. When Big Show got back to his feet, Austin cut him down again with a pair of Stunners, then invited all the WWE Superstars to the ring to celebrate with the troops.

RHODES SCHOLAR

Steve Austin didn't learn this until later in life, but his mother, the late Beverly Williams, went to Arlington Heights High School with Virgil Runnels. He was a few grades ahead of her, and she told her son that he was a good football player.

For those still working on their degree in the subject of sports entertainment, Virgil Runnels was the son of a plumber who became an in-ring icon known as The American Dream, Dusty Rhodes.

THESE NUMBERS ARE "STUNNING"

When most people consider Steve Austin's in-ring success, they often think about Stone Cold's dominant run in WWE. However, "Stunning" Steve Austin's combined championship tenure in WCW runs more than 100 days longer than The Texas Rattlesnake's combined title reigns in WWE. Stone Cold was recognized as a WWE Champion (529), Intercontinental Champion (64), and World Tag Team Champion (141) for 734 days. "Stunning" Steve was recognized with the WCW World Television Championship (431), WCW U.S. Heavyweight Title

(240), and WCW/NWA Tag Team Championship (168) for a combined total of 839 days.

AUSTIN'S INJURY, COMPRESSED

The storyline that saw Stone Cold run over by a mystery assailant's vehicle at *Survivor Series* in 1999 was one created out of necessity. Two years after being incapacitated by a botched piledriver at *SummerSlam*, the nagging pain Steve Austin felt daily was intensifying. He was suffering from central cord compression, as the piledriver forced years of sports-related bone spurs to start growing into the congenitally narrow spinal cord Austin had been born with.

With his muscles rapidly deteriorating, Austin's only alternative was to have his C3 and C4 vertebrae fused. Though he was a viable candidate for a three-level fusion, going that route would have ended Austin's career. The surgery was a success, but it was nearly a year before Stone Cold could compete again. And he'd do so against the man who ran him down, Rikishi.

The Texas Rattlesnake has said on several occasions that even though he thought the hit-and-run wasn't a great angle, it did the trick and bought him the time he needed to recover.

WHAT ROCK
TOLD AUSTIN

"I'm sitting up, and I sit next to him as he's lying there, in front of everybody, and I whispered to him, 'I thank you so much for everything that you've done for me.' And I said, 'I love you.' And I heard him say, 'I love you, too.' I hit him on the chest and I left. Left him in the ring. That was it, and he retired that night."

The Rock's March 28, 2020, Instagram post reveals what he told Stone Cold after pinning him in their *WrestleMania XIX* match

BROKEN SKULL RANCHER

In 2006, a friend contacted Steve Austin about a secluded, 2,000-acre ranch just outside Tilden, TX. Though he resided in Los Angeles, Austin, a lifelong hunter, dreamed of one day owning a ranch in the South Texas region. Enamored with the location's Nueces River frontage, various terrain changes, and deer stand layout, he decided to buy it and called it the Broken Skull Ranch, referencing the name of his customized WWE Championship. As he once wrote on his site, "Hey, I had to break my skull to buy this place. I wanted the name to be a reflection of a dream realized that was made possible by my lifelong passion and love for the business of professional wrestling."

The 1,500-plus mile commute between Los Angeles's Marina del Rey community and Tilden prompted Austin and his wife to sell the Tilden ranch in 2017. They soon found a new location in Nevada, about 50 miles out from Reno, and called it the Broken Skull Ranch 2.0.

WELCOME TO HALL, STONE COLD

On April 4, 2009, Mr. Vince McMahon inducted Stone Cold Steve Austin into the WWE Hall of Fame. Austin was the prestigious hall's 62nd inductee, and he entered it in true Stone Cold fashion: By bashing and downing a few Steveweisers in front of WWE's Superstars and members of the WWE Universe inside Houston's Toyota Center.

1:81

A HARD PLACE FOR ROCK

U ntil *Survivor Series* in November 2001, The Rock had never scored a pinfall or submission victory over Stone Cold Steve Austin. In a four-year drought that started at *In Your House: D-Generation X* in December 1997, The Great One's only victories over the Rattlesnake came via disqualification, until Kurt Angle betrayed Austin and Team Alliance in a 5-on-5 Winner Take All Elimination Match. That gave The People's Champion a much-needed opening to Rock Bottom Austin and score the three count.

1:82

STONE COLD ADAM COLE?

O n the June 10, 2020, episode of Austin Creed's popular *UpUpDownDown* gaming series on WWE's YouTube channel, former NXT Champion Adam Cole revealed that he was a huge fan of Stone Cold Steve Austin while growing up. In fact, in high school, he shaved his head bald and wore a gold chain, just like The Texas Rattlesnake. Cole's admission and high school photo left Creed (aka Xavier Woods), Cesaro, and Tyler Breeze . . . stunned.

And if that isn't enough, Cole's real name is *Austin* Jenkins.

1:83

TWO GIANT LOSSES

WCW's *Clash of the Champions XX*, emanating from Atlanta, GA's Center Stage Theater on September 2, 1992, marks the end of "Stunning" Steve Austin's second reign as WCW World Television Champion, as well as the final televised U.S. appearance of Andre the Giant. WWE's larger-than-life Hall of Famer passed away on January 27, 1993.

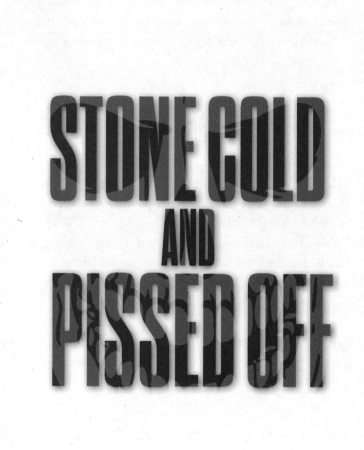

"This belt is mine! This belt is mine! I am a fighting champion! I am a man's man! I am a champion of champions, and I will put this belt on the line! Listen to me! Listen to me because this is extremely important. I will put this belt on the line to anybody . . . anybody back there in the dressing room! But I just won't do it tonight in this piece of crap town! No-no-no, I won't do it in this piece of crap town, because you don't deserve to see Stone Cold Steve Austin in action, and that's all I got to say about that!"

The radically changed WWE Champion tells the WWE Universe in Anaheim, CA's Arrowhead Pond exactly what he thinks of them (*SmackDown*, May 24, 2001)

THE GOING GETS *TOUGH ENOUGH*

After a several-year hiatus, *WWE Tough Enough* returned to television in 2011, and Stone Cold Steve Austin took the helm for his first foray as a reality TV host. Joined by trainers Trish Stratus, Booker T, and Bill DeMott, plus guests like The Rock, John Cena, and Rey Mysterio, Austin put 14 men and women through rigorous training and challenges, eliminating competitors one by one until one person earned themselves a WWE contract.

The season's winner, Andy Leavine, was officially initiated into the world of sports entertainment with a slap in the face from Vince McMahon, followed by a Stone Cold Stunner from the Rattlesnake.

AUSTIN'S FAVORITE *WRESTLEMANIA* ENTRANCE

Stone Cold's *WrestleMania 13* entrance, in which he walks through breaking glass just as his theme kicks in, is a favorite on many Top 10 *WrestleMania* entrance lists. Steve Austin remembers it fondly as well, but it isn't his favorite. Austin believes the greatest entrance in the history of The Show of Shows belongs to Triple H. At *WrestleMania X-Seven*, The Cerebral Assassin headed to the ring while Lemmy and Motörhead performed his entrance theme, "The Game," live in Houston's Reliant Astrodome.

A VERY SORE LOSER

During his November 2019 interview with Undertaker on *Steve Austin's Broken Skull Sessions*, Austin shared some painful memories with The Phenom. He first brought up their 1989 match in Memphis, when Undertaker was the masked menace known as The Punisher. The two had agreed earlier that The Punisher would call the match, but when he tried calling high spots, Austin couldn't hear what he was saying. After three vain attempts, The Punisher stopped trying and started beating down Austin, hard. The Rattlesnake cites his being hard of hearing in one ear as another reason why he learned to call his own matches — it proved less painful for him in the long run.

Another time, Austin and Undertaker were supposed to ride together to a venue in Tennessee, except they couldn't because they were supposed to be opponents in a Six-Man Tag Team Match that night. Austin joked that The Punisher better watch out because he intended to stretch him, meaning he'd dominate him with painfully stiff holds. That didn't sit well with The

Punisher, who was also goaded further by Dutch Mantell to put a hurting on Austin. Battered again throughout that match, Austin never joked like that with him again.

1:88

WATCH YOUR BACK

While Stone Cold Steve Austin defended his WWE Championship inside New Jersey's Continental Airlines Arena at *King of the Ring* (June 24, 2001), WCW Champion Booker T emerged from the crowd and attacked The Bionic Redneck. Moments later, he sidewalk-slammed Austin through the announcers' table.

Years later, Booker told Austin on his podcast that he had been later informed he had broken the Rattlesnake's hand. Austin set the record straight and confirmed that was not the case. He also revealed that when he flat-backed onto the table, he bounced off onto an announcer's chair, breaking three transverse processes in his back. Austin assured Booker he was in no way responsible for that, either.

1:89

REMEMBER THE ALAMODOME

Stone Cold's first Royal Rumble Match victory occurred not only in his home state of Texas, but before a capacity crowd of

60,477. The 1997 *Royal Rumble* inside San Antonio's Alamodome drew the largest live attendance ever for a *Royal Rumble* event and, as of this writing, ranks 23rd among all WWE pay-per-view attendance records.

LOST IN VESTMENT

To this day, Stone Cold Steve Austin is pissed off at himself about *WrestleMania XV*. Though he defeated The Rock to win his third WWE Championship at The Showcase of the Immortals, he committed what he considers to be a cardinal sin in sports entertainment: He forgot to pack one of his black vests before heading to Philadelphia's First Union Center. Austin had no choice but to come out for the main event in one of his Stone Cold T-shirts.

"Here you are, the biggest stage of all, in a high-profile match, *The Rock* as your opponent . . . and I gotta go out there in a rinky-dink-ass T-shirt," Stone Cold recalled on his podcast *The Steve Austin Show*. "I kicked myself in the ass over and over *and over* again about that particular night."

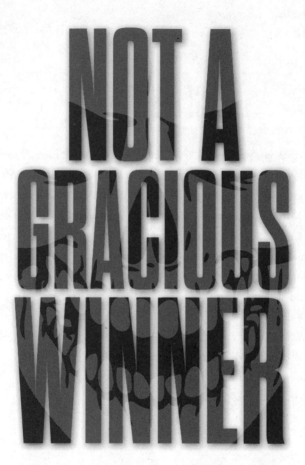

"Let me tell you something, Ricky Steamboat. I don't have to tell the world you're one of the greatest champions to ever set foot in the ring. But let me tell you something right now, you mealy mouthed Hawaiian punk! You saved yourself one hell of an ass-kickin'!"

"Stunning" Steve Austin rubs it in Ricky Steamboat's face after "The Dragon" forfeits his WCW United States Heavyweight Championship due to injury (*WCW Fall Brawl: War Games*, September 18, 1994)

FULLY LOADING

Operating a cement mixer on Mr. McMahon's Corvette, a crane to destroy the DX Express, and a forklift to flip over Triple H's car — with him in it — came pretty naturally to Stone Cold Steve Austin. Back during his days at the University of North Texas, his football team's defensive line coach found him a job at Watkins Motor Line, where he'd utilize heavy machinery to work on the freight dock and load and unload trucks. Austin held the job at Watkins full-time after leaving college and enrolling in "Gentlemen" Chris Adams's wrestling school.

STONE COLD'S MOST IMPORTANT CHAMPIONSHIP

Of all his championships, the one that means the most to Stone Cold Steve Austin is the Intercontinental Title he won at *SummerSlam* in 1997. He appreciates that particular championship belt's rich history of previous owners, including Randy Savage, Ultimate Warrior, and Mr. Perfect. Furthermore, Austin acknowledges that even though everyone wants to win a world title, the Intercontinental Championship is considered the "workhorse title" of sports entertainment. The fact that he almost broke his neck winning it made it even more significant to him.

Vince McMahon suggested that Austin just have another Intercontinental Title made when he expressed his desire to keep it. After Austin explained why that championship belt meant so much to him, the WWE Chairman was fine with letting him have it.

1:94

AUSTIN'S FAVORITE *WRESTLEMANIA* MATCH (THAT WASN'T HIS OWN)

Stone Cold has cited several times, in numerous interviews and on his podcast, that his all-time favorite match is "Macho Man" Randy Savage and Ricky "The Dragon" Steamboat's Intercontinental Championship bout at *WrestleMania III*.

Like many of the 93,000-plus fans that attended the Pontiac Silverdome on March 29, 1987, Austin considers the in-ring chemistry between Savage and Steamboat to be "off-the-charts good." Add to that the battle's "realistic" intensity and a secondary storyline involving Miss Elizabeth and George "The Animal" Steele, and he believes the match was ahead of its time.

TWICE BLESSED(?) WITH *NO MERCY*

The Bionic Redneck main-evented in a WWE Championship Anything Goes Match on not one, but *two* pay-per-views called *No Mercy* in 1999. At the first one, a U.K.-exclusive event broadcast from the Manchester Evening News Arena in England on May 16, Stone Cold Steve Austin successfully defended the title in the no-disqualification, foreign objects-allowed bout against challengers Undertaker and Triple H. When *No Mercy* made its U.S. debut in Cleveland, OH's Gund Arena on October 17, The Texas Rattlesnake was the challenger and The Game was the champion in the hellacious main event, which ended when The Rock accidentally blasted Austin with Triple H's sledgehammer. This particular *No Mercy* marked the last pay-per-view Austin would compete in for a year due to needing neck surgery.

"I'm supposed to face Sycho Sid tonight, and some guy, a 350-pound buffoon that calls himself 'Gorilla Monsoon, the Commissioner,' says, 'No, no. Sycho Sid is at home with a concussion.' Sycho Sid may be at home with a concussion and an icepack on his head, but he's also got a yellow stripe runnin' right down the middle of his back. As far as Gorilla Monsoon goes, I got a big bunch of bananas, and I can tell you where to stick each and every one of 'em!"

The Texas Rattlesnake spews his venom toward WWE Commissioner Gorilla Monsoon (*Raw*, January 27, 1997)

AUSTIN AND BISCHOFF, REUNITED

Eric Bischoff must have wondered how he and Stone Cold Steve Austin, the man he fired via phone and FedEx nearly eight years earlier, would interact when they met in February 2003. The storyline called for now-*Raw* General Manager Bischoff to locate Stone Cold — who had been absent from WWE for a time — and re-sign him to a WWE contract, or find himself on the unemployment line. Though Bischoff wouldn't find Austin in Bandera, TX, during the February 3 episode of *Raw*, the Rattlesnake did pull the former WCW president over to one side to talk. There, Austin assured Bischoff that his dismissal from WCW was in the past, and that he was willing to wipe the slate clean and work together. The two share an amicable relationship to this day.

THE TENNESSEE SPUD

Steve Austin's early days wrestling in Memphis with the United States Wrestling Association were often lean ones. He and his USWA peers joked that Tennessee was the "Nutrisystem Territory," since they'd all lose so much weight there. Austin's grocery shopping list consisted primarily of a bag of potatoes, as many cans of tuna fish as he could afford, and disposable razors. When he ran out of tuna fish, he'd spend three or four days eating nothing but raw potatoes, since he didn't have a stove to cook anything.

1:99

"STONE COLD STEVE AUSTIN, NUMBER ONE"

Though The Rock and The Texas Rattlesnake have enjoyed a close friendship over the years, The People's Champion has admitted several times that the two were fiercely competitive about claiming the top spot in WWE during its Attitude Era. During their WWE Championship Match buildup to *WrestleMania XV*, Austin once signed an autograph for The Great One as "Stone Cold Steve Austin, Number One." Rock initially thought his rival was joking, then realized that he was likely signing all of his autographs that way. It bothered him to no end, but he knew the only way he could start signing in that fashion was to beat Austin in the ring.

2:00

WATCH AND LEARN

Early in Steve Austin's USWA career, the promotion's booker, "Dirty" Dutch Mantell, once chewed out the rookie for having little to no idea how to do anything in a match beyond executing moves. Mantell showed Austin how to put a headlock on an opponent in a way that he could hear the opponent communicate with him. After that, he ordered the young novice to sit in the venue's doorway and study every match until he learned the nuances to performing in the ring. Mantell's teachings that day motivated Austin throughout most of his career to observe every match at events where he appeared.

2:01

NO LONGER FEELING DEFLATED

Nearly 22 years after a live *Raw* segment showed Stone Cold invading the Walton, KY, home of Brian Pillman, Steve Austin finally apologized for his actions that prompted Pillman to defend his family with a 9 mm pistol. He made the apology on Twitter (@steveaustinBSR) to Brian Pillman *Jr.*, who was only three years old when his turtle-shaped kiddie pool was destroyed during The Texas Rattlesnake's invasive rampage.

"Young man, I was just taking care of bizness," Austin replied on February 19, 2018, following Pillman Jr.'s facetious tweet that Stone Cold had "belligerently destroyed" his property. "I did what I had to do. I apologize for damaging your little swimming pool."

Austin reiterated his regret when Pillman Jr. was a guest on his podcast *The Steve Austin Show*. Pillman Jr. laughed and accepted the apology, especially after Austin agreed to send over a six-pack peace offering of his Broken Skull IPA.

KEEP IT BASIC AND BLACK

The Ringmaster debuted in 1996 wearing emerald green ring trunks and the same white boots with stars that "Stunning" Steve Austin wore in WCW. WWE had originally wanted Austin to wear an emerald green singlet, but he emphatically shot down that suggestion right away.

When Austin got the green light to develop his Stone Cold identity, he collaborated with WWE seamstress and costume designer Terry Anderson. Together, they decided to keep Stone Cold's entire look basic, and in Austin's favorite color. That meant black trunks, black boots, and black athletic tape, eventually followed by the black vest and black knee braces.

STONE COLD'S *WRESTLEMANIA* REGRET

Steve Austin considers his *WrestleMania X-Seven* No Disqualification Match against The Rock to be one of his personal two favorite matches . . . with the exception of the ending. According to Austin, his one regret was accepting a beer from Mr. McMahon, shaking his hand, and turning against the WWE Universe.

Stone Cold had originally thought turning into WWE's top villain would help keep his character from becoming stale.

However, when he heard 67,925 fans cheering in his home state as he beat The Rock with a steel chair that the Chairman had given him, he wanted to call an audible. Though he enjoyed the longest WWE Title reign of his career and it opened up creative new ways to build on his character (including the "What?" chant), Austin wishes he hadn't sold his soul to the proverbial devil.

2:04

ENTER "THE DRAGON"

WCW championship gold was often at stake between future WWE Hall of Famers Steve Austin and Ricky Steamboat. The Dragon ended "Stunning" Steve's second reign as WCW World Television Champion at *Clash of the Champions XX* (September 2, 1992) and his first as WCW U.S. Heavyweight Champion at *Clash of the Champions XXVIII* (August 24, 1994). Austin, meanwhile, captured unified WCW/NWA Tag Team gold as a Hollywood Blond alongside "Flyin'" Brian Pillman when they defeated Steamboat & Shane Douglas on *WCW Worldwide* March 27, 1993. At *WCW Fall Brawl: War Games* (September 18, 1994), Austin became a two-time WCW U.S. Heavyweight Champion (albeit for a very brief time) after an injury forced The Dragon to relinquish the title.

AUSTIN'S LADY, JEANIE

Less than a year after Steve Austin made his wrestling debut (as Steve Williams) against Frogman LeBlanc, he and the journeyman grappler met again in the squared circle for *USWA Championship Sports* on April 21, 1990. It was there that Austin introduced "the sexiest girl in America, the gorgeous and lovely Jeanie." It was quickly revealed that she was Jeanie *Adams*, former wife of Austin's mentor, "Gentleman" Chris Adams.

In the months that followed, "Lady Jeanie" accompanied Austin to the ring as they engaged in a fierce rivalry with Adams and his new wife, Tori. Jeanie joined Austin as Lady Blossom when he headed to WCW in 1991, and the two married the following year.

UNBEATEN STREAKS SNAPPED

Savio Vega has the distinction of handing both Steve Austin and The Rock their first singles losses on WWE programming. On the April 13, 1996, installment of *Superstars of Wrestling*, Stone Cold (though still managed by The Million Dollar Man), having declined a match with Vega, was caught off-guard with a rollup from a masked unknown called "The Caribbean Kid" . . . who promptly revealed himself as Vega. On *Raw* exactly 366 days later,

Vega grabbed a handful of tights to pin then-unbeaten Superstar Rocky Maivia.

AUSTIN LOSES HIS HARLEY

The Hollywood Blonds might not have existed if "Stunning" Steve Austin had been given a choice. In January 1993, he was excited by WCW's promise of a huge singles push with ring legend Harley Race as his manager. That changed at a WCW TV taping (Austin believes it was in either Dothan, AL, or Columbus, GA), when Brian Pillman approached Austin and suggested that they start thinking of a finishing move since they were now a tag team.

Pillman's news caught Austin completely by surprise, and he wasn't happy about it. He went to WCW's booker, Dusty Rhodes, who confirmed that there had been a change in plans. Rhodes also assured that he and "Flyin'" Brian were a team that had legs.

A NOT-SO-*GREAT AMERICAN BASH*

The July 14, 1991, edition of *The Great American Bash* was not the WCW pay-per-view debut Steve Austin could have possibly envisioned. WCW's new World Television Champion and

Terrance Taylor faced "Beautiful" Bobby Eaton & P.N. News in the event's first contest, a Capture the Flag Scaffold Match (dubbed "The Skywalkers II" in reference to a previous Scaffold Match at *Starrcade* 1986). The "capture the flag" stipulation was a last-minute addition to the tag team bout for good reason: The wrong kind of scaffold had been erected that night. Piping at the bottom was too big for the competitors to wrap their hands around and suspend themselves from the scaffold, which hung more than 20 feet over the ring. It also didn't help that the 403-pound P.N. News was fighting on a thin, shaky platform that looked barely able to support all four competitors.

No one was knocked off the scaffold, though Austin & Taylor lost the match after Eaton captured their flag and walked back to his end of the platform. The bout and the pay-per-view were universally panned by critics, and though he had nothing to do with the stipulations or faulty framework, Austin regards it as one of the worst matches of his career. If that isn't enough, *The Great American Bash* marked not only Austin's WCW pay-per-view debut, but also Eric Bischoff's. It almost makes one forget that Ric Flair jumped over to WWE with the WCW Title just weeks before he was to defend it against Lex Luger at this pay-per-view.

2:09

"STARSTRUCK" STEVE AUSTIN

Stone Cold isn't the type to be "starstruck" by anyone. Neither is Steve Austin, with one notable exception: Bunny Martin, who was 16 years old when he won the World Yo-Yo Championship in Toronto, Canada, had come to Edna, TX, to perform at Austin's school. Sixth-grader Austin approached Martin for his signature after the show, and he still has the autograph to this day.

2:10

A TITLE CHANGE ON THE "HOUSE"

Out of 27 *In Your House* events during a near-four-year span, a new WWE Champion was crowned only once. (No new champion was declared at *Breakdown: In Your House* in September 1998.) And, of course, Stone Cold Steve Austin put himself in the hunt.

At *In Your House: Final Four* (February 16, 1997), The Texas Rattlesnake battled Bret Hart, Vader, and Undertaker in a Four Corners Elimination Match for the title, which had been vacated by Shawn Michaels only days before. The Hit Man won the WWE Championship, sending Undertaker over the top rope to eliminate him after the already-ousted Austin had distracted The Phenom from the outside.

2:11

NO WAY *OUCH*

To save his job, *Raw* General Manager Eric Bischoff had to face Stone Cold in a match at *No Way Out* (February 23, 2003).

Days earlier, while the two discussed their bout over a phone call, Steve Austin wanted Bischoff to understand that since he had been absent from WWE for seven months, his timing in the ring might be off. However, he promised that he had no plans to intentionally hurt the *Raw* GM because of their history at WCW.

When *No Way Out* emanated from the Bell Centre in Montreal, Canada, Jim Ross's comment as Austin headed to the ring perfectly summed up the events that were about to transpire: "My God, he came to whip another man's ass!" Stone Cold did just that, delivering three Stunners to pin the *Raw* GM (though, with a little assistance from Austin, he kept "kicking out" of the Rattlesnake's pinfall attempts). Once Austin's hand was raised in victory, he celebrated with a fourth Stunner to Bischoff. All we can say is, it's a good thing Austin wasn't out to intentionally hurt Bischoff.

2:12
AUSTIN'S PINK AND BLACK ATTACK

There was a different look to Stone Cold Steve Austin when he and WWE Champion Shawn Michaels locked up in Kuwait City on May 12, 1996: The Texas Rattlesnake modified his all-black ring gear to include neon pink tape around his arms and wrists. Austin had borrowed Bret Hart's pink tape to have some fun and get a reaction out of The Showstopper. It was the type of gag WWE's Superstars often played on each other while overseas.

"WHOOP-ASS" GRANDMA

At the 1998 *Royal Rumble* Truck Giveaway Sweepstakes, grandmother Mildred Bowers of suburban Nashville, TN, was announced as the winner of a badass Stone Cold pickup vehicle. The specially equipped black Chevrolet Z71 pickup sported a Stone Cold skull on the hood and a tailgate that said "100% Pure Whoop-Ass!" Ms. Bowers opened up a can and gave the truck to her teenage grandson, who was a fan of The Texas Rattlesnake.

GUY'S A NIGHTMARE TO WORK WITH

Before their first USWA match together in Memphis, TN, "Nightmare" Danny Davis said he'd listen to Steve Austin call the bout. The surprised Austin had expected the ring veteran to do it so he could learn from him, but Davis said he trusted the rookie and would only chime in as needed. Austin's experience with the future founder and former owner of Ohio Valley Wrestling (OVW) gave him the confidence to call the vast majority of his matches throughout his career.

BACK TO HIS COUNTRY ROOTS

Following the enormously successful *Steve Austin's Stone Cold Metal* one year earlier, Mars Entertainment Corp. collaborated with The Texas Rattlesnake on a country compilation album in the fall of 1999. Sporting a lenticular CD case that morphed Austin's face into that of a rattlesnake, *Steve Austin's Stone Cold Country* collected 14 songs from country music's greatest, all personally handpicked by The Bionic Redneck.

Track listing:
- "I've Always Been Crazy" — Waylon Jennings
- "Fire and Smoke" — Earl Thomas Conley
- "The Ride" — David Allan Coe
- "I Take a Lot of Pride in What I Am" — Merle Haggard and The Strangers
- "Love a Little Stronger" — Diamond Rio
- "Yard Sale" — Sammy Kershaw
- "Midnight in Montgomery" — Alan Jackson
- "Let Go of the Stone" — John Anderson
- "Highway 40 Blues" — Ricky Skaggs
- "Some Girls Do" — Sawyer Brown
- "That's My Job" — Conway Twitty
- "Don't Take Her She's All I Got" — Tracy Byrd
- "I've Got Rights" — Hank Williams Jr.
- "Whiskey River" — Willie Nelson

AND THE OSCAR FOR "BEST STUNNERED SUPERSTAR" GOES TO . . .

In July 2017, The Rock provided his motivation behind his now-legendary flops around the canvas after eating a Stone Cold Stunner. On his Twitter account (@therock), The People's Champion stated that he and Steve Austin would bet cases of beer over how crazy Rock could sell The Texas Rattlesnake's finisher. As Austin has repeatedly mentioned that no one sold the Stunner better than The Most Electrifying Man in All of Entertainment, we can hazard a guess that The Rock has a well-stocked bar at home.

WHO SUGGESTED AUSTIN'S SMOKING SKULL WWE TITLE?

The Smoking Skull WWE Championship is definitively "Stone Cold." Its genesis, however, was the result of a conversation Steve Austin had while hanging with The Road Warriors (or Legion of Doom, you decide). With The Toughest S.O.B. in WWE having become a household name in 1998, Hawk and Animal suggested that Austin start coming out to the ring with his own belt and have the title sport a skull that definitively stated who its owner was.

AUSTIN VS. CHYNA?

There was a very real possibility that The Ninth Wonder of the World would challenge Stone Cold for the WWE Championship at *SummerSlam* in 1999. Chyna had already achieved historic firsts by competing in that year's Royal Rumble Match and King of the Ring Tournament. She officially became the title's top challenger after substituting for the incapacitated WWE Champion and winning a No. 1 Contender's Match against Undertaker and Triple H (with a little help from The Texas Rattlesnake, who returned to Stunner The Game and rolled her onto him for the pinfall).

Sadly, her historic bid for the WWE Title ended a week later, after Mankind beat her in a match to take the No. 1 Contender spot. When a controversial decision added Triple H into the mix, Austin's *SummerSlam* title defense turned into a Triple Threat Match that Mankind won.

"Everybody talks about 'The Best There Is, The Best There Was . . .' all the other crap! 'The Excellence of Execution' . . . Bret [Hart], clichés are clichés, and an ass-whippin' is an ass-whippin'! And that's *exactly* what you're gonna get tonight at the hands of Stone Cold Steve Austin!"

Stone Cold bottom-lines it for Bret Hart before heading to the ring for their match at *Survivor Series* (November 17, 1996)

HANDPICKED BY THE HIT MAN

It was during a match with Shawn Michaels that Steve Austin earned the respect of Bret Hart. Austin was only days away from forever shedding his Ringmaster gimmick when he lost a match to The Heartbreak Kid at the Houston Summit on March 9, 1996. After the bout, the then-WWE Champion Hit Man approached Austin, told him he had a great match, and that he'd work with him anytime.

Austin recalled that night while talking with Hart on WWE Network's *Steve Austin's Broken Skull Sessions*, as he felt it led to a big moment in his career. After months away from WWE, The Excellence of Execution could have faced anyone on the roster for his in-ring return at *Survivor Series 1996*. He handpicked "Stone Cold."

MILKIN' IT

Celebrated portrait photographer Annie Leibovitz shot more than 180 ads for the National Milk Processor Education Program's iconic "Got Milk?" campaign. The campaign featuring celebrities from all walks of life — wearing milk moustaches, naturally — included Stone Cold, whom Leibovitz photographed in 1999. "[Leibovitz] made me look like a Greek god," Steve Austin recalled in a June 2018 interview with *Fast Company*, referring to the way she handed him two glasses of milk to hold near his waist and look like he'd bash them together the way he would his Steveweisers.

On a side note, on the very same day Leibovitz photographed the Rattlesnake, she also shot a world-famous, talking frog named Kermit.

2:22

PWI POWERHOUSE

Throughout his career, Stone Cold Steve Austin earned a spot in the illustrious *Pro Wrestling Illustrated*'s (*PWI*) monthly Top 10 rankings 70 times. In the annual *PWI* 500 rankings, The Texas Rattlesnake finished No. 1 in 1998 and 1999, and No. 2 in 2001. Bret Hart (1993–94), Shawn Michaels (1996–97), John Cena (2006–07), and Seth Rollins (2015, 2019) also claimed the top spot on two occasions, while Cena added a third No. 1 ranking in 2013.

2:23

TAKING ONE ON THE CHIN

The "Highway to Hell" brought Stone Cold Steve Austin and Undertaker into New York City's Madison Square Garden for *SummerSlam* August 30, 1998. The Texas Rattlesnake successfully defended his WWE Championship in a hellacious battle with

The Deadman, though some of the details how may still be fuzzy for Austin, since he got knocked out early in the bout.

While countering Undertaker's attempted backdrop with a kick to the midsection, The Phenom unexpectedly shot back up. The back of his head connected with Stone Cold's chin, knocking Austin loopy and sending him straight down to the canvas. Austin woke up a few seconds later, but he needed the referee to remind him where he actually was.

2:24

"YOU WANT SOME KETCHUP WITH THAT ASS-WHOOPING?"

"Attention, shoppers, there's cans of whoop-ass in Aisle 2! That's Aisle 2!"

Supermarket savagery was in great supply during the December 13, 2001, edition of *SmackDown*. That's when Stone Cold pummeled Booker T up and down the aisles of the Green Frog Market, a Bakersfield, CA, grocery store that first opened its doors in 1934. Though the market closed in 2013, memories of the fracas remain everlasting, as Steve Austin assaulted the six-time World Champion with hilarious one-liners as well as nuts, potatoes, beans, oranges, coffee . . . anything that was within arm's length.

According to both Superstars, the fight was heavily ad-libbed as they went, and they estimate that they caused more than

$10,000 in damages to the store. It's a safe bet that neither had coupons to help with some of the cost.

"Price check on a jackass!"

"STUNNING" WCW THEMES

"Stunning" Steve Austin's first WCW entrance theme was hardly the sound of breaking glass and harmonic discourse that eventually accompanied his Stone Cold persona. From 1991 until 1993, Austin headed ringside to Tele Music's "A Roman Love (I)," a bombastic musical piece that evoked classic cinema more than hell-raisin' antihero.

In 1993, Austin changed his tune to "Satan's Sister," a theme by Chris Goulstone and Bosworth Backgrounds that was made popular during "Stunning" Steve's time with fellow Hollywood Blond, "Flyin'" Brian Pillman.

"Sportsmanship? What a load of *crap*. Don't preach
your morality to me. Steve Austin doesn't have any
compassion. You want mercy? Take your ass to church."

A Stone Cold promo that extols the
virtues of WWE's Attitude Era (1998)

FIRST ISN'T ALWAYS BEST

The first WWE Superstar to eat a Stone Cold Stunner is a tricky question. Steve Austin connected with the Stunner to Jason Arhndt (aka Joey Abs from Shane McMahon's Mean Street Posse) on the June 10, 1996, installment of *Superstars of Wrestling*, which was recorded from the North Charleston Coliseum in South Carolina on May 28. On *Raw* June 17, the Rattlesnake struck with a Stunner to Savio Vega, advancing past the King of the Ring quarter finals inside Fayetteville, NC's Cumberland County Memorial Auditorium. However, that match was recorded on May 27, technically making Vega the inaugural recipient of Austin's finisher.

STONE COLD MEETS THE TERMINATOR

AT-800 altered *SmackDown* history at the Baltimore Arena in Maryland November 11, 1999. Newly crowned by Mr. McMahon as "Box Office Champion of the World," guest commentator Arnold Schwarzenegger lent a helping hand — and a steel chair — to special match enforcer Stone Cold Steve Austin. The Rattlesnake used the chair to terminate Triple H's shenanigans and give Test the win in an Eight-Man Tag Team Elimination Match.

The Game confronted Schwarzenegger after the match, only to take a further beatdown that had him seeing the end of days (also the name of the film Schwarzenegger was starring in at the time). Austin's and Arnold's paths would cross again more than a decade later, when the two starred in *The Expendables*.

UP TO THE CHALLENGE

On July 6, 2014, *Steve Austin's Broken Skull Challenge* premiered on CMT. The reality competition show, set in an Agua Dulce, CA–based representation of Austin's Broken Skull Ranch, pitted eight male and female contestants of varying athletic backgrounds against each other in extremely grueling physical challenges in the dry desert heat. The last one standing would face the toughest challenge in the form of an excruciating obstacle course called the Skullbuster, designed by Austin himself and modified at the start of every season.

Broken Skull Challenge was a champion on CMT's lineup for five seasons, with the last ending in December 2017. In 2015, the series also won in its second nomination of a Directors Guild of America Award for Outstanding Directing — Reality Programs.

WEDDED BLITZ

On the November 29, 1999 edition of *Raw*, Triple H interrupted Stephanie McMahon and Test's wedding ceremony and showed video footage of himself marrying a seemingly unconscious Stephanie at the Little White Wedding Chapel's drive-thru Tunnel of Love in Las Vegas. The world-famous chapel has performed wedding nuptials for many renowned celebrities and athletes, including Frank Sinatra, Michael Jordan, Paul Newman and Joanne Woodward, Sylvester Stallone, Jim Ross, and Stone Cold Steve Austin.

"Shawn, I know you're at your house doin' push-ups, sit-ups, jumpin' jacks, whatever you gotta do, gettin' on some stupid machine, to get your ass ready for *WrestleMania XIV*. At the Boston Fleet Center, son, I'll tell you this: When best meets best, when Stone Cold meets The Heartbreak Kid, I want you to be at your best, because an ass-whoopin' is always the same, no matter how good a shape you're in.

"As far as Mike Tyson is concerned, you're hired on to be the enforcer, so that's exactly what you'll be as long as you do what you're supposed to do. You stick your little nose in my business and it's like I said before: I'll take that gold tooth, knock it out of your head, and I'll make a necklace, a bracelet, a ring . . . whatever I wanna make out of it.

"*WrestleMania XIV*, March 29. Austin. Michaels. Tyson. The sh*t's on, and that's the bottom line, 'cause Stone Cold said so!"

Stone Cold issues warnings to Shawn Michaels and "Iron" Mike Tyson heading into *WrestleMania XIV* (*Raw*, February 16, 1998)

A STONE COLD V.I.P.

Steve Austin's first foray into non-WWE television programming was on the syndicated action-comedy series *V.I.P.*, starring Pamela Anderson. (Remember her at *Royal Rumble* 1995 and *WrestleMania XI*?) In the episode "Scents and Sensibility" (October 24, 1998), Austin plays himself and he's under the protection of bodyguard Nikki Franco (Natalie Raitano). While Stone Cold teaches Nikki how to perform a piledriver(!), she says, "It must be awesome being a pro wrestler!" Austin casually replies, "It's pretty cool. I got a couple of action figures."

THE END OF THE HOLLYWOOD BLONDS

There seem to be several factors that contributed to the breakup of The Hollywood Blonds. First, despite being a heel tag team, "Stunning" Steve Austin & "Flyin'" Brian Pillman's ring chemistry and promos — particularly their "Flare for the Old" mockups of Ric Flair and Arn Anderson — had earned them a growing fan base. Reportedly, that irritated WCW management, which told the tandem that they simply weren't winning over crowds.

A July 2018 edition of Eric Bischoff's *83 Weeks* podcast indicated that the decision was more financially motivated than talent oriented. The former WCW president explained that the organization was in a cost-cutting phase, so it made more economic sense for WCW to have two higher-paid athletes work individually in separate storylines rather than together on one.

Regardless of the reasoning, the decision to break them apart was ultimately the same. On *WCW Saturday Night* October 30, 1993, Colonel Robert Parker approached Austin to congratulate him on his singles match victory. He also disrespected Pillman, who was recuperating from a leg injury, and suggested that "Flyin'" Brian be put down like a racehorse. Pillman started to attack Parker until "Stunning" Steve assaulted Pillman from behind. Severing all ties with his now-former partner, Austin became part of Colonel Parker's Stud Stable and an eventual WCW U.S. Heavyweight Champion. Sadly, The Hollywood Blonds were no more.

2:34

SUPERSTAR INK

The Toughest S.O.B. in WWE has two tattoos on his left leg. Steve Austin was around 25 when he got the first one: A skull, located midway between his calf and ankle. Years later, after feeling homesick while living in Villa Rica, GA, he decided to get a Texas tattoo with a Texas Longhorn skull in the center. Austin had the state portion colored in red later on, as he thought the previous artist didn't produce a geographically accurate rendition of the Lone Star State. At one point he considered getting ink on his arms, but ultimately decided he didn't want tattoos that were heavily visible.

2:35

CHALLENGING THE STATUS QUO

There were two occasions when a new WWE Champion was crowned *after* Stone Cold Steve Austin had already won his title opportunity at *WrestleMania*. On February 15, 1999, Austin defeated Mr. McMahon in a Steel Cage Match at *St. Valentine's Day Massacre* to secure a *WrestleMania XV* title opportunity against then–WWE Champion Mankind. On January 21, 2001, The Texas Rattlesnake won his third Royal Rumble Match to earn a *WrestleMania X-Seven* title bid against then-WWE Champion Kurt Angle. Unfortunately for Mrs. Foley's baby boy and the Olympic Hero, they each fell to The Rock, who entered both *WrestleMania*s as the champion.

2:36

STEVE AUSTIN'S MANAGER ... PAUL BEARER?

At various points throughout 1998 and 1999, Steve Austin lost the WWE Championship to Undertaker, Kane, and Dude Love, all of whom were at one point managed by Paul Bearer. Interestingly, Austin was also managed by Bearer, back when he was Percival Pringle III and the two were a part of WCCW. "Stunning" Steve also tag-teamed with Pringle on a few occasions, causing mayhem together against the likes of Chris Von Erich and "Gentlemen" Chris Adams.

2:37

EXIT "THE DRAGON"

Most fans reference Ricky Steamboat's storied rivalry with Ric Flair. However, "The Dragon's" last match before retiring came against another longtime rival, "Stunning" Steve Austin. At *Clash of the Champions XXVIII* (August 24, 1994), Steamboat rallied to defeat "Stunning" Steve for the WCW United States Heavyweight Championship at the Five Seasons Center in Cedar Rapids, IA.

Sadly, Steamboat's victory came at a cost. He suffered a severe back injury during the match, and it ultimately forced him to forfeit the title back to Austin at *WCW Fall Brawl: War Games* on September 18. The two would share a sports-entertainment stage again 15 years later, when both Austin and Steamboat were inducted into the WWE Hall of Fame's Class of 2009.

IT'S IN HIS HEAD

Not surprisingly, WWE Superstars accrue a lot of cuts, bruises, and even the occasional scar from their in-ring matchups. Stone Cold was no exception. To this day, he owns a particularly noticeable scar right on the back of his head, near the occipital knob, thanks to a chair-wielding Mr. McMahon at *No Mercy* in October 2001. The scar might look cleaner had it been closed up by stitches instead of staples, but Steve Austin wears it like a badge of honor. (Plus, he gave the WWE Chairman more than a few stitches of his own.)

"I'm the kind of person that I'm gonna work my ass off for you, no matter what it is. If it's a physical job or whatever, I'm the guy for the job. If you hire me for somethin', I'm gonna bust my ass for you, okay? I've done that my whole life, whether it's workin' for the highway department, workin' on a freight dock, whatever. But when I feel like someone's startin' to poke me with a stick, that's when you're startin' to piss me off. And I felt like after everything that happened to me in WCW, bein' fired by that injury and bein' prodded and someone sayin' basically, 'Nah, you're not marketable, you're not gonna be successful,' I really got a damn attitude.

"I was a guy that was always on time for work. I never played like I was hurt; if I was hurt, I was hurt. If I was sick, I was sick. But when you start f*ckin' with me, I'm gonna bite your ass. That's been my attitude kinda my whole life, but I just had to get that chip on my shoulder in this business for me to really succeed, and get kicked down enough times and get f*cked over enough times that I said, 'Y'know what? I'm gonna do this. I'm gonna do it my way. I *can* do it my way, and if you get in my way, I'm gonna run your ass over."

Excerpt from *Steve Austin: Bottom Line* on WWE Network

THE PAY-PER-VIEW "CORE FOUR"

Starting with 1998's *Royal Rumble*, every WWE pay-per-view main event up until the U.K.-exclusive *Rebellion* in October 2002 featured Stone Cold, The Rock, Triple H, and/or Undertaker — a total of 66 consecutive pay-per-views. Not including *Rebellion*, the streak would have continued up until *WrestleMania XIX* in March 2003.

BRACED FOR (ALMOST) ANYTHING

At the main event of 1999's *SummerSlam* — a Triple Threat Match with Mankind and Triple H — WWE Champion Stone Cold Steve Austin wore matching knee braces for the first time. Unfortunately, he wasn't used to having two. During the match, while guest referee and former Minnesota Governor Jesse "The Body" Ventura directed his attention toward Shane McMahon on the outside floor, Austin got himself tangled up in the ropes. Ventura didn't hear Austin call out to him for help, so it took The Game to help free The Texas Rattlesnake while he attacked him. It's entirely possible that he may have also been laughing a little while doing so.

STUNNERS FOR EVERYONE!

On *Raw* July 16, 2001, Steve Austin literally floored seven members of the invading Alliance with Stone Cold Stunners, seemingly to build momentum for Team WWE going into *InVasion*. But seven Stunners wasn't his personal best. Back on *Sunday Night Heat* June 6, 1999, The Texas Rattlesnake connected with *eight* consecutive Stunners, striking Superstars, referees, WWE personnel . . . pretty much anyone within his reach. In fact, those eight joined the four Stunners he had delivered to various Superstars earlier that evening, bringing his total to a whopping 12 Stunners in one night.

Stone Cold: You're about to hand this man, The Undertaker, a championship match after *Backlash*.

Crowd: *What?*

Stone Cold: That's what you're doin'.

Crowd: *What?*

Stone Cold: That man right there.

Crowd: *What?*

Stone Cold: A championship match.

Crowd: *What?*

Stone Cold: After *Backlash*.

Crowd: *What?*

Stone Cold: Why?

Crowd: *What?*

Stone Cold: 'Cause he deserves it?

Crowd: *What?*

Stone Cold: 'Cause he's got that stupid bandana?

Crowd: *What?*

Stone Cold: Those stupid tattoos?

Crowd: *What?*

Stone Cold: Those stupid gloves?

Crowd: *What?*

Stone Cold: Those stupid pants?

Crowd: *What?*

Stone Cold: Those damn boots?

Crowd: *What?*

Stone Cold [*to Flair*]: Does he scare you?

Crowd: *What?*

Stone Cold: Does he make you shake?

Crowd: *What?*

Stone Cold: Are you intimidated?

Crowd: *What?*

Stone Cold: Is he special?

Crowd: *What?*

Stone Cold: Are you scared?

Crowd: *What?*

Stone Cold: Is it because he's got "Deadman" on his shirt?

Crowd: *What?*

Stone Cold [*to Undertaker*]: What does that mean?

Crowd: *What?*

Stone Cold: 'Cause you're dead?

Crowd: *What?*

Stone Cold: You don't breathe?

Crowd: *What?*

Stone Cold: You got no pulse.

Crowd: *What?*

Stone Cold: You're not alive.

Crowd: *What?*

Stone Cold: You bought the farm.

Crowd: *What?*

Stone Cold: You bit the big one.

Crowd: *What?*

Stone Cold: You kicked the bucket.

Crowd: *What?*

Stone Cold: You think you're special?

Crowd: *What?*

Stone Cold: You deserve a championship match? *Why?*

Crowd: *What?*

Stone Cold: I wanna know why.

Crowd: *What?*

Stone Cold: Because you ride that stupid bike?

Crowd: *What?*

Stone Cold: I'll get on that son of a bitch . . .

Crowd: *What?*

Stone Cold: . . . kickstart it . . .

Crowd: *What?*

Stone Cold: . . . and ride that son of a bitch as long as I want to!
[*Crowd cheers.*] Ric, you know what my watch is tellin' me?

Crowd: *What?*

Stone Cold: Do you know what this son of a bitch is sayin'?

Crowd: *What?*

Stone Cold: It's talkin' loud and clear.

Crowd: *What?*

Stone Cold: And I can hear it.

Crowd: *What?*

Stone Cold: I ain't got no hearin' aids.

Crowd: *What?*

Stone Cold: I got no problem.

Crowd: *What?*

Stone Cold: It's sayin' . . .

Crowd: *What?*

Stone Cold: . . . it's time . . .

Crowd: *What?*

Stone Cold: . . . for Ric Flair . . .

Crowd: *What?*

Stone Cold: . . . to make a decision.

Crowd: *What?*

Stone Cold: Look at me!

Crowd: *What?*

Stone Cold: When I talk to ya!

Crowd: *What?*

Stone Cold: Is it gonna be . . .

Crowd: *What?*

Stone Cold: . . . Stone Cold?

Crowd: *What?*

Stone Cold: Stone Cold.

Crowd: *What?*

Stone Cold: Stone Cold!

Crowd: *What?*

Stone Cold: *I said, "Stone Cold!"* [*Crowd cheers.*] Or is it gonna be The Undertaker . . .

Crowd: *What?*

Stone Cold: . . . The Deadman . . .

Crowd: *What?*

Stone Cold: . . . in that championship match . . .

Crowd: *What?*

Stone Cold: . . . after *Backlash?*

Crowd: *What?*

Stone Cold: I think you need to make up your mind.

Crowd: *What?*

Stone Cold: Right now.

Crowd: *What?*

Stone Cold: Thank you.

Crowd: *What?*

Stone Cold: You're welcome.

Crowd: *What?*

> The Texas Rattlesnake questions Undertaker's
> demand that WWE co-owner Ric Flair put
> him in a WWE Undisputed Championship
> Match at *Backlash* [*Raw*, April 8, 2002]

CRASHING THE SET

On the unforgettable evening when Stone Cold drove a Coors Light beer truck down to the ring (*Raw*, March 22, 1999), he figuratively brought the house down. He almost did likewise in the literal sense with the entire TitanTron. The massive beer rig was so large that it didn't clear the structure, and it very nearly pulled down the *Raw* set.

According to Stone Cold, they didn't do a practice run beforehand, and he felt he was in too deep to turn the truck back after hitting the WWE structure. Fortunately, the TitanTron stayed up, and Austin delighted the WWE Universe as he used a high-powered firehose (also for the very first time) to douse The Rock, Mr. McMahon, and Shane McMahon with countless gallons of beer.

STONE COLD AUTHOR

Nearly seven months after stepping into the ring for one last match, The Toughest S.O.B. in WWE officially became an author. Co-written with Dennis Brent and Jim Ross, *The Stone Cold Truth*, an autobiography focusing on Austin's life and in-ring career, was published on October 28, 2003. The book debuted on the New

York Times Best Seller Nonfiction list at No. 11 on November 16 and climbed as high as No. 8. Austin enjoyed similar success on the Publishers Weekly Bestsellers Nonfiction list, reaching No. 10 in December 2003.

2:46

"Well, since he is still breathin', if you want me to finish this can of whoop-ass, gimme a 'Hell, yeah!'"

Stone Cold asks the WWE Universe if he should let Mr. McMahon be stretchered out or continue to beat on him at *St. Valentine's Day Massacre: In Your House* (February 14, 1999)

VARIATIONS ON A THEME

Since late 1996, the WWE Universe has identified the sound of glass breaking with the arrival of Stone Cold. However, his entrance music has changed over the years. From October 1996 until October 1998, The Texas Rattlesnake headed ringside to Jim Johnston's "Hell Frozen Over." He next came out to the similar sounding "I Won't Do What You Tell Me" until September 2000, when he switched over to Disturbed's popular "Glass Shatters" theme.

Multiple Jim Johnston themes were experimented with during the latter half of 2001, including "Rattlesnake" (used only once on July 23), "Paranoid," and "Venomous." Another song — "Unbreakable," by Johnston and Cage9 — was used primarily at WWE live events. Ultimately, "I Won't Do What You Tell Me" would return at the end of the year, and it has remained Austin's entrance theme to this day.

SNAKES? WHY DID IT HAVE TO BE SNAKES?

Long before Steve Austin became The Texas Rattlesnake, he was nearly bitten by one. Austin was about 12 years old and throwing bales of hay from the second floor of his family's barn when he noticed the reptile only inches away from his arm. He instinctively tossed himself out the barn's open second-story bay door to escape.

Years later, Austin drew inspiration from his harrowing experience and added that fearful element to his ever-evolving Stone Cold persona. Though he made himself unpredictable and biting like a rattlesnake, Austin feels no love for the creatures when he sees them slithering around Broken Skull Ranch.

2:49

STUNNING RESILIENCY

It took nearly six months before a WWE Superstar took a Stone Cold Stunner and managed to kick out of a pinfall attempt. Following a long sabbatical away from WWE, Bret "Hit Man" Hart returned at *Survivor Series 1996* and, despite being caught flush with a Stunner, denied what looked like certain victory for The Toughest S.O.B. in WWE. Not to be outdone, Austin pulled off a remarkable feat of his own by escaping The Excellence of Execution's go-to finisher, the Sharpshooter.

AUSTIN GETS SHORTY

Shortly before *WrestleMania X-Seven* commenced in Texas's Space City, Stone Cold and independent furniture retail giant Jim McIngvale tag-teamed at a steer auction at the Houston Livestock Show and Rodeo, where they paid a then-record $600,000 on its grand champion, Shorty. Purchased from his 11-year-old owner, Zane Hayes, the white and orange-spotted bovine didn't go home with either Steve Austin or the business mogul known throughout Texas as "Mattress Mack." Instead, he was served up to charity as the "guest of honor" at the 17th annual Thomas Law Enforcement Wild Game Cook-Off, which benefited the Houston Farm & Ranch Club Bear Creek youth center. He was some pretty pricey ground round.

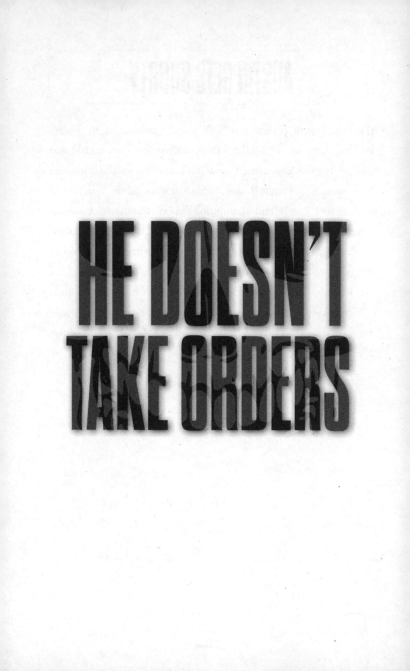

2:51

"You sit here and you say, 'That's an order!' 'This is an order!' 'That's an order!' Hell, I can look at you, son, and the only thing you can order is a whole bunch of cheeseburgers!"

The Texas Rattlesnake's biting comments to WWE Commissioner Slaughter, who ordered the injured Stone Cold to relinquish his Intercontinental Championship to the winner of an Intercontinental Title Tournament at *Badd Blood* (*Raw*, September 8, 1997)

OFF THE CUFF ASS-WHOOPIN'

At *WrestleMania 32* (April 3, 2016), 101,763 members of the WWE Universe erupted when Attitude Era alumni Stone Cold Steve Austin, Shawn Michaels, and Mick Foley headed to the ring in Dallas's AT&T Stadium. There, the trio pummeled the League of Nations, with The Texas Rattlesnake delivering Stone Cold Stunners to Rusev and Bad News Barrett. After being coaxed into dancing with Xavier Woods, Austin Stunnered the New Day Superstar as well.

What no one realized at the time is that Stone Cold opened up those cans of whoop-ass with a torn right rotator cuff. After injuring himself while training for *WrestleMania 32*, MRIs revealed that he had a rotator cuff tear, bicep tendinosis and instability, AC joint arthrosis, and a degenerative labral tear. Austin underwent surgery shortly after his appearance at The Showcase of the Immortals, but he certainly affirmed that, even years after his retirement, he was still The Toughest S.O.B. in WWE.

WHAT'S IN A NUMBER?

The number 27 ranks among the most coveted of entry spots in WWE's annual 30-Man Royal Rumble Match. As of this writing, four WWE Superstars have won the contest from the No. 27

position — more than any other number. It's the first number to produce multiple Royal Rumble Match victors (Big John Studd in 1989, Yokozuna in 1993) as well as back-to-back winning entrants (Yokozuna in 1993, Bret Hart in 1994). Stone Cold Steve Austin was the last No. 27 entrant to win in 2001, though in 1998 he won his second Royal Rumble Match from the No. 24 spot. No. 24 is currently tied with No. 30 (and No. 28, if you add in the Women's Royal Rumble Match) for the second highest number of Rumble winners. (Each has won three times.)

2:54

WIDESPREAD DEVASTATION (INC.)

Long before Steve Austin joined the Dangerous Alliance or the Stud Stable at WCW, he was briefly associated with Devastation Inc. at WCCW/USWA. Austin, "Gorgeous" Gary Young, Jeff Gaylord, and Sheik Braddock were managed by General Skandor Akbar, who oversaw several incarnations of the longstanding faction. Other Devastation Inc. members at various points in time included The Missing Link, Greg Valentine, Kamala, Abdullah the Butcher, Ted DiBiase, Cactus Jack Manson, and a pre-Undertaker Punisher.

Austin spent a lot of time on the road traveling with Akbar and Bronco Lubich, a longtime WCCW referee and former tag partner of Angelo Poffo, Randy Savage's father. He valued his travels with Akbar and Lubich, and in his autobiography he credits them for teaching him about ring psychology and respecting the business.

A PHENOM-ENAL GESTURE

With Stone Cold Steve Austin's popularity on the rise in 1996, WWE management decided to produce a T-shirt. On an episode of WWE Network's *Undertaker: The Last Ride*, Steve Austin recalled that he had pitched a basic black T-shirt saying "Austin 3:16" on the front, while the back sported a human skull with the words "Stone Cold" carved into its forehead. WWE Chairman Vince McMahon was hesitant to sign off; he felt the skull was closer to Undertaker's intellectual property, but if Austin had The Phenom's blessing, he would approve it as well.

Austin approached The Deadman and explained the idea for his shirt, adding that he understood if there was any issue. Undertaker simply replied, "Yeah, man. Go for it."

A March 1999 article in *Forbes* reported that WWE sold more than 12 million "Austin 3:16" shirts in 1998 alone, with Stone Cold merchandise accounting for half of WWE's total merchandise sales.

A QUEST FOR THE CUP

Between *Survivor Series 1996* and *WrestleMania 13* in 1997, Bret Hart and Stone Cold Steve Austin clashed in the final of the

1996 Middle East Cup Tournament, which took place in Dubai, United Arab Emirates, on December 2. The result that night was the same as the two classic pay-per-view confrontations it was sandwiched between, with The Excellence of Execution emerging triumphant over The Texas Rattlesnake.

To get to the Hit Man in the finals, Austin advanced past two future rivals that were also instrumental to his career. He defeated Owen Hart in the quarterfinals, then bested Undertaker in the semi-finals.

2:57

FIRST DAY ON THE JOB

One week after Linda McMahon appointed Stone Cold Steve Austin her successor as WWE's CEO — in response to her husband revealing himself as The Corporate Ministry's "Greater Power" — The Texas Rattlesnake had a busy first day on the job in WWE's headquarters in Stamford, CT. (And yes, this was the actual headquarters.) As seen on *Raw* June 14, 1999, the Stone Cold CEO:

- commandeered Mr. McMahon's private parking space
- instructed the lobby receptionist to answer phones with "Who the hell is this?" and "What the hell do you want?"
- had Mr. McMahon's personal assistants bring him cold beer and a Crown & 7 at 10 a.m.
- held a boardroom meeting where he fired a VP for

looking stupid, promoted a mailroom clerk to bring him beer, and declared a beer-drinking contest to weed out weaker executives

- instructed one HR specialist to bring him some beer and trained another to learn all things Stone Cold
- ordered an accountant to transfer some zeroes from Mr. McMahon's salary over to Mick Foley's, and turn Shane McMahon's salary into Austin's beer budget
- filled the Chairman's office with cow manure

2:58

A CHAMPIONSHIP STAT 4 X 4

Stone Cold Steve Austin not only won four championships in 1997, he was also stripped of them all that same year. An injury to Shawn Michaels forced Austin to relinquish his first World Tag Team Championship. Despite promptly winning it back with Dude Love, his injury at *SummerSlam* required him to surrender it anew. The injury at *SummerSlam* also meant having to forfeit his first Intercontinental Title. Then, a few weeks after winning it back at *Survivor Series*, Austin gave it up a second time, simply because he wanted to piss off Mr. McMahon, kick The Rock's ass, and focus on the WWE Championship.

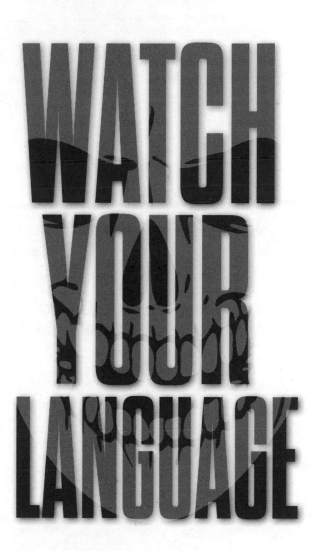

"I got to apologize for my language. Usually, it's a lot worse than this, but I'm tryin' to mind my manners."

Stone Cold's color(ful) commentary after cursing out Mick Foley during a No. 1 Contender's Match between Foley and Terry Funk (*Raw*, May 4, 1998)

SENTIMENTAL VALUE

In 1993, Brian Pillman emphasized to "Stunning" Steve Austin the importance of making The Hollywood Blonds stand out in WCW's Tag Team division. So the duo invested in matching ring gear and innovated distinct actions like their "Brush with Greatness," in which they'd film each other perform power moves with an imaginary hand-cranked camera. Pillman also urged that their characters should wear gold chains and he gave one to Austin. Stone Cold wore it throughout his WWE career, not only because it was the look back then but because of the sentimental value it had after Pillman's passing. To this day, he keeps the gold chain locked up inside a Fort Knox vault in his garage.

KISS THAT SINGING CAREER GOODBYE

When Steve Austin was a teenager, he wanted to be a wrestler and a rock star. After multiple failed attempts to learn how to play guitar, Austin decided he'd just be a front man for whatever band he was part of. Being a huge KISS fan, he once put on a set of headphones and started belting out "Shock Me" — until his brother Kevin suddenly slapped the headphones off his head. Kevin told Austin in no uncertain terms that he wasn't very good, and that he should listen to himself without the headphones. Austin gave it a try and . . . well, he went on to have a very successful career in sports entertainment. We'll leave it at that.

DÉJÀ VU

The severe neck injury Stone Cold suffered from a sit-down piledriver at *SummerSlam 1997* is eerily similar to what happened to New Japan Pro-Wrestling star Masahiro Chono almost five years earlier. During his NWA World Heavyweight Title defense on September 23, 1992, Chono was injured after taking a sit-down piledriver. Though he won the bout, the injury to his neck was serious enough to eventually prompt Chono to alter his ring technique.

Chono's opponent that night in Japan's Yokohama Arena? WCW's "Stunning" Steve Austin.

MONSTER TRUCK MISHAPS

For years, Stone Cold Steve Austin wreaked havoc on WWE programming with little to no prior training operating vehicles like a Zamboni, a cement mixer, and an ambulance. Driving a 2,000-horsepower, methanol/alcohol-fueled monster truck with four-wheel drive over The Rock's new Lincoln Continental in April 1999, however, was one of his bigger — and more dangerous — challenges.

Austin learned to drive the "Austin 3:16"-themed monster truck in the parking lot for about 15 minutes before *Raw* emanated from Grand Rapids, MI. However, while he sat inside the vehicle in a holding garage and waited to receive a cue that signaled the end of *Raw*'s commercial break, the truck's exhaust fumes nearly overpowered him. With his eyes watering badly and almost unable to breathe, Austin nearly exited the vehicle to get some air when he received the go-ahead to crush The Rock's car.

Destroying the Lincoln was easy enough, as was driving the monster truck onto a carpeted entranceway inside the Van Andel Arena. Unfortunately, Austin revved up the engine so much that when he hit the accelerator, the vehicle's wheels spun out and yanked up 50 feet of carpet from beneath the truck. Stone Cold thought he had scared a nearby cameraman who went flying; the truth is he was standing on the carpet and it shot out from under him.

2:64

STUNNING THE LESSER OF TWO EVILS

The September 16, 1999, edition of *SmackDown* was the first time the WWE Championship changed hands on the blue brand, and it was all because of Stone Cold Steve Austin. Seeing that Mr. McMahon was the enemy of his current enemy, then-champion Triple H, Austin intervened in The Game's match with the Chairman. Delivering Stone Cold Stunners to both Triple H and Chyna, Austin pulled the battered McMahon onto the fallen Game to get the three count. It was Mr. McMahon's first and only WWE Championship, which he vacated the following week on *Raw*.

2:65

AUSTIN SHOOTS *STRAIGHT UP*

On August 12, 2019, *Straight Up Steve Austin* premiered on USA Network. The unique interview format brings Austin and a guest to a different city around the country each week, where the two engage in custom adventures and share stories about their respective careers. The first season featured guests such as actor/comedian Rob Riggle, *Impractical Jokers'* Sal Vulcano, Cleveland Browns quarterback Baker Mayfield, Becky Lynch, funnyman Gabriel "Fluffy" Iglesias, country superstar Trace Adkins, and NASCAR great Dale Earnhardt Jr. *Straight Up Steve Austin's* second season began airing in January 2021.

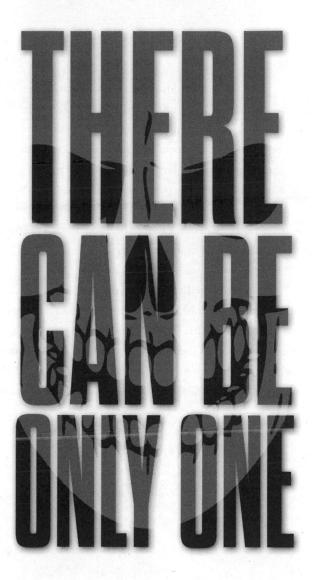

"Without gettin' overly sentimental, I'll go on the record as sayin' every single time that I've been in the ring with The Rock, he has brought out the absolute best in Stone Cold Steve Austin. So, when I roll into the Astrodome and *WrestleMania* on April 1 . . . do I want to beat you, on a personal level? Oh hell, yeah, I do. But on a professional level, which bleeds over in my personal existence, I *need* to beat you, Rock. I need it more than anything that you could ever imagine.

"So that's the mentality I roll into the Astrodome with, the fact that Stone Cold Steve Austin is back, and that I must beat The Rock to be the [WWE] Champion once again, and there is no other way. There can be only one. There can be only *one* [WWE] Champion. And that will be, Rock, when it's all said and done, Stone Cold Steve Austin. With all due respect."

Stone Cold Steve Austin's final thoughts
during a sit-down interview with Jim Ross
and The Rock, ten days before *WrestleMania*
X-Seven (*SmackDown*, March 22, 2001)

AUSTIN'S GO-TO GUY

WWE's road agents help run a show or event, act as liaisons between Superstars and management, and assist Superstars in determining the best ways of entertaining the WWE Universe. Jack Lanza, a former World Tag Team Champion as one half of The Blackjacks, was supportive of Stone Cold Steve Austin when he started at WWE, reassuring him that he was on the right path toward winning over the WWE Universe. For the vast majority of Stone Cold's matches in WWE, Lanza was his go-to road agent.

ONE OF THE BEST NICKNAMES IN HISS-TORY

"Rattlesnakes don't make good corporate pets!" — **Jim Ross**

Stone Cold Steve Austin credits WWE Hall of Famer Jim Ross for coming up with the Texas Rattlesnake moniker on commentary. Many fans reference good ol' J.R.'s line about rattlesnakes not making good corporate pets from *Raw* March 30, 1998. However, he first described Austin as having "the personality of a rattlesnake" at *King of the Ring* on June 8, 1997, during Stone

Cold's match against his co-World Tag Team Champion, Shawn Michaels. Ross thought the term really captured the essence of Austin's evolving in-ring mannerisms, mindset, and motivation.

CHAMPIONSHIP MONOPOLIZER

It's rare enough when a WWE Superstar holds two championships simultaneously. Stone Cold Steve Austin did so on *three* occasions. He and Dude Love were already World Tag Team Champions when Austin won his first Intercontinental Title in 1997. The following year, Austin was WWE Champion when he and Undertaker captured the World Tag Team Titles. Stone Cold was WWE Champion again when he and Intercontinental Champion Triple H secured World Tag Team gold in 2001.

HIS WCW IN-RING DEBUT

"Stunning" Steve Austin's first official match in WCW was against Chuck Coates on *World Championship Wrestling*, broadcast June 1, 1991. Accompanied to the ring by Vivacious Veronica, Austin made short work of Coates, a journeyman sports entertainer who also occasionally appeared on WWE programming. "Stunning" Steve also debuted his finisher, the Stun Gun, which prompted commentator Jim Ross to say, "A real *stunner*, right there."

"JAKE CAGE" IS ON THE CASE

S teve Austin had made a few appearances on television, primarily playing himself in cameos, before appearing on the CBS police procedural series *Nash Bridges* in February 1999. Starring Don Johnson as the titular San Francisco police investigator, the series introduced Austin as tough-as-nails Detective Jake Cage in the season 4 episode "Pump Action."

Johnson's bodyguard, a WWE fan, had recommended that Johnson offer Austin a role as a one-off bit part. The *Nash Bridges* crew liked working with Stone Cold so much, however, that they wrote his character into more episodes. Jake Cage would appear in six episodes between the series' fourth and fifth seasons in 1999 and 2000, and CBS even approached Austin about a Jake Cage spin-off series. The Texas Rattlesnake declined, citing that he had asses to whoop back in WWE.

RING, RUMBLE, REIGN

Stone Cold is the second of six Superstars to win a King of the Ring Tournament, a Royal Rumble Match, and a World Championship. Bret Hart preceded Steve Austin, while Triple H, Brock Lesnar, Edge, and Sheamus followed The Texas Rattlesnake. Austin is the only Superstar in this group to win his first WWE Championship *after* winning the King of the Ring Tournament and a Royal Rumble Match.

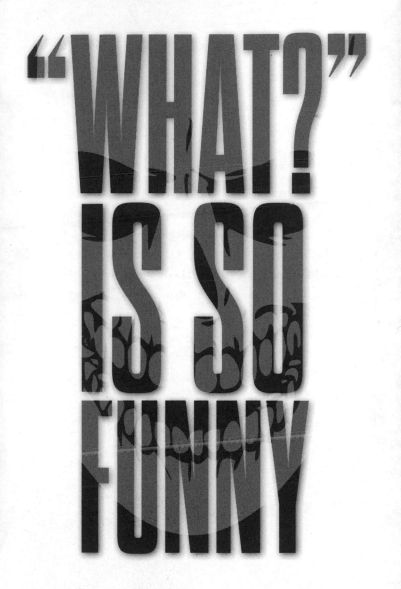

"Look at ya! You're 275 pounds! Your name is Hugh. Morrus. *What?* Your name is Hugh Morrus. *What?* Is that funny? Is that . . . *humorous?* Are you here to make me laugh? *What?* You're pathetic! Look at me! *You're pathetic!* Y2J whipped your ass! I'm ashamed of ya! Step back!"

Hugh Morrus isn't laughing about becoming a casualty of Stone Cold Steve Austin's inaugural "What?" rant (*Raw*, August 13, 2001)

HIGH PRAISE, INDEED

While a guest on *Busted Open* in September 2019, Steve Austin's all-time favorite ring legend, Ric Flair, cited only three men as sports entertainment's biggest stars: Hulk Hogan, Undertaker, and Stone Cold Steve Austin. Said the former 16-time World Champion and two time WWE Hall of Famer, "Steve, in my estimation, will always be the biggest star in the history of the business."

BLOOD ON THEIR HANDS

Most WWE Universe members associate *WrestleMania 13* with the iconic image of blood pouring down Stone Cold's face as he struggled to free himself of Bret Hart's Sharpshooter. It turns out that went against WWE's PG rating and strict "no blood" policy, meaning that Superstars couldn't deliberately "get color." The Hit Man thought their Submission Match really needed it, however, especially if Steve Austin was to pass out in the Sharpshooter rather than submit. Hart assured the Rattlesnake that he would take the blame for any fallout backstage, and they went through with it without getting approval beforehand.

Though WWE management was far from thrilled about seeing Austin bleed profusely onto the canvas, no one could argue

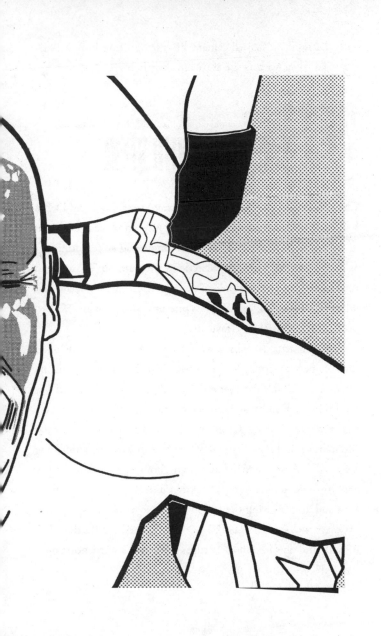

with the result. It helped cement Hart's transition into WWE's top villain and Austin's rise as the unlikely hero.

2:76

SING ALONG WITH STEVE

The classic backstage vignettes featuring Stone Cold and Debra, Kurt Angle, and Mr. McMahon in July 2001 were born out of necessity. Both Steve Austin and Angle had suffered injuries at *King of the Ring*, but they needed to remain on TV to build toward their confrontation at *SummerSlam*. Therefore, the duo locked up over weeks of hilarious one-upmanship in an effort to become Mr. McMahon's "favorite."

The segments — which were mostly ad-libbed — included each Superstar trying to out-hug Mr. McMahon; Austin's attempt to soothe the stressed-out Chairman with an off-key rendition of "Kumbaya," followed by the Olympic Hero's equally cringeworthy "Jimmy Crack Corn"; and Stone Cold gifting McMahon and himself legit cowboy hats, plus a tiny kiddie one for Angle. (Austin actually found and bought Angle's hat at the San Antonio International Airport.) The Olympic Hero tried his hand at gift-giving the following week with cowboy badges for everyone (except Debra). His effort earned the Rattlesnake's disdain and the response, "Badges? We don't need no stinkin' badges!"

WHAT DRIVES THE RATTLESNAKE?

If you thought Stone Cold was unpredictable in the ring, you should check out what's in Steve Austin's garage. It's an eclectic collection of vehicles to say the least. Among a few of his "sweet rides" are his McLaren 720S, a 2019 white Corvette (no cement poured into this one), a 1955 Buick Special, and a 1974 Z-28 Chevy Camaro. For off-road terrain, Austin has 4x4 vehicles like his Jeep, a 1988 Dodge Ramcharger, and a plethora of ATVs, quads, and off-road bikes, mostly of the Kawasaki variety.

For basic, everyday travel, the Rattlesnake relies on his go-to 1995 Ford Bronco XLT, his 2016 Range Rover, a 2003 Ford Focus and Chevrolet Silverado Z71, and a 1996 Chevrolet Suburban. Oh, and did we mention he also has a jet ski and a private plane? He's certainly come a long way from the vehicle he learned to drive in, his mom's 1978 Buick Century wagon. You'll often find Austin tinkering with his vehicles on his Instagram (@steveaustinbsr).

WHERE THERE'S A SMOKING SKULL . . .

Why did Stone Cold have a Smoking Skull WWE Championship commissioned less than four months after he was presented with WWE's newly designed title? Quite frankly, Steve Austin didn't like the new title. As he went to deliver a Stone Cold Stunner to Mr. McMahon on *Raw* March 30, 1998, a sharp, jagged edge on one of the championship's plates cut his chin.

In reality, Mr. McMahon was none too pleased with the smoking skull design Austin had commissioned without the Chairman's authorization. The fans loved it, however, and it was eventually decided that the custom title could be worked into storylines. Austin's Smoking Skull WWE Title was quietly retired a year later, after the Rattlesnake lost the championship at *SummerSlam*.

2:79

VEST TO IMPRESS

Steve Austin's black entrance vests are a Stone Cold staple, the genesis of which he has long credited to WWE seamstress Terry Anderson. His initial vest, first seen before his match with Undertaker on *Raw* July 29, 1996, featured a winged Stone Cold logo and star on the back. Future iterations, however, quickly evolved after Anderson developed a method of burning glue onto leather, then using a plumbers candle to apply the right amount of wax onto the burned area.

The seamstress created many memorable vests for Austin. The backs of them sported human or rattlesnake skulls and various phrases like "100% Whoop Ass." The fronts generally featured a combination of "Austin," "SCSA," "3:16," and various phrases made of three different letters — among them, "DTA" ("Don't Trust Anybody"), "SOB" ("Son Of a Bitch"), and "BMF" (please don't make us say it). The last one he wore for *WrestleMania XIX* said "OMR." When it was revealed that was his last match, it became clear that the letters stood for "One More Round."

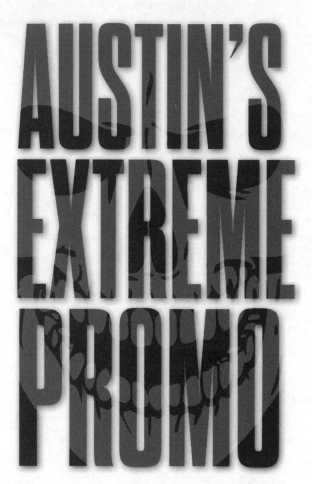

"I stroll into the ECW Arena . . . it's the biggest piece of crap I've ever seen! . . . You got a bunch of damn *misfits*, runnin' around thinkin' that they can actually wrestle. All I've seen in ECW is a bunch of violent crap, and that's exactly what I'll call it because that's what it is.

"Steve Austin is here to wrestle. It's what I do best. It's what I do better than anyone in the world.

"'Stunning'? Tossed it out the window. Never was meant to be. ECW's gonna find out firsthand what Steve Austin can do. And I'm gonna show everybody here exactly what a *true* superstar is supposed to do, what a true superstar is supposed to *be*. Because no one here can hold me back. Not Tod Gordon. Not Hulk Hogan. Not Eric Bischoff. Nobody. I'm gonna be the superstar that I always knew that I could be, because there's no one — *no one* in ECW that can stop me."

After recalling his dismissal from WCW, "The Extreme Superstar" Steve Austin warns he can't be held back anymore (*ECW Hardcore TV*, October 10, 1995)

AS CLOSE TO AUSTIN VS. HOGAN AS WE'LL EVER GET

One of sports entertainment's greatest dream matches, Stone Cold Steve Austin vs. Hulk Hogan, never became a reality. However, the Rattlesnake and the Hulkster *did* mix it up one time inside the ropes. The two were in opposing corners on *Raw* March 11, 2002, when Austin & The Rock battled the New World Order's "Hollywood" Hogan, Scott Hall, & Kevin Nash in a Three-on-Two Handicap Match. Their in-ring exchange in Detroit's Joe Louis Arena was minimal and fairly even, though Hogan powered the nWo to victory with the legdrop onto The People's Champion. In addition to this being the first and only match involving both Superstars, this bout marked the first time the nWo competed together in a WWE ring.

E-LIMO-NATING OBSTACLES

On *Sunday Night Heat* January 24, 1999, Mr. McMahon took steps to ensure that Stone Cold had "No Chance in Hell" of winning that year's Royal Rumble Match. From Anaheim, CA's Arrowhead Pond, the Chairman challenged Steve Austin to meet him inside the ring. However, he had ordered the arena's VIP parking lot reserved for limousines only and barricaded the entranceway to prevent the Rattlesnake from entering. At least, he *thought* he did.

Mr. McMahon hadn't expected Stone Cold to return inside the "Limonator," a white, 400-horsepower, two-wheel-drive hybrid of a limousine and monster truck. Austin simply drove his leviathan-sized vehicle over the barricade and straight onto several parked cars, then headed into the arena.

2:83

WE'LL MAKE THIS QUICK

Making his *WCW Clash of the Champions* debut at the General James White Memorial Civic Auditorium and Coliseum in Knoxville, TN (June 12, 1991), "Stunning" Steve Austin defeated "Jumpin'" Joey Maggs in a blink-and-you'll-miss-it time of 25 seconds.

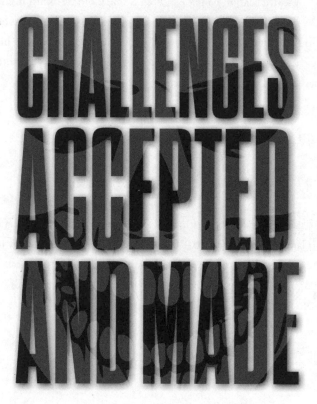

CHALLENGES
ACCEPTED
AND MADE

"You got your little challenges, you think you're all big
and tough. You stand up there all jacked up. I got a
couple of challenges for you: I challenge you to get
you a decent haircut. Since you're a piece of crap, I
challenge you to flush yourself down a commode!

"As far as you or anybody else is concerned, all you got to do
is sign a damn piece of paper, and I'll beat the hell out of
anybody, right here in the middle of the ring. So, you're damn
right, you got your shot. You understand what I'm sayin'? But
you don't suck because these people say you suck. You suck
because Stone Cold said so. And that's the bottom line!"

One night after winning back the Intercontinental
Title, The Texas Rattlesnake responds to a new
challenge made by The Rock with some interesting
challenges of his own (*Raw*, November 10, 1997)

FIRST BEER TASTING?

E CW's *November to Remember*, which took place November 18, 1995, inside Philadelphia's ECW Arena, is particularly memorable for two reasons: First, it was "The Extreme Superstar" Steve Austin's first time competing for the ECW World Heavyweight Championship. Second, it was the first time we saw him drink a beer in any arena. In this instance, Austin did it to mock ECW's beer-guzzling Sandman, whom he had just decimated and replaced in the title match.

A STUNNER OF A REQUEST

M ore than 80,000 fans in Detroit's Ford Field watched as guest referee Steve Austin delivered a Stone Cold Stunner to Donald Trump at *WrestleMania 23*. Austin's finisher came while the future POTUS celebrated his "Battle of the Billionaires" victory over Mr. McMahon. It was an unbelievable *WrestleMania* moment, though *how* that moment came to fruition is equally fantastic.

During multiple interviews, Austin recalled that on the day of *WrestleMania 23* (April 1, 2007), Vince McMahon himself suggested that Trump let Stone Cold hit him with the Stunner. Though one of his aides balked at the suggestion and urged him to decline, Trump said that if it would help the show, he'd do it. Stone Cold went over the move with him and, to Trump's credit — as well as the great delight of the WWE Universe — he took the Stunner. At least he still had his hair by the end of the night . . . unlike Mr. McMahon.

A SLOW DEMISE FOR THE DX EXPRESS

Blowing up the DX Express on *SmackDown* April 27, 2000, is regarded as one of Stone Cold's most unforgettable moments of destruction in WWE. However, it was almost unforgettable for the wrong reasons. On his podcast series *The Steve Austin Show*, Austin recalled operating the "Austin Deconstruction" crane with no issues during rehearsal. Unfortunately, he wasn't aware that someone had raised the crane arm entirely before the *SmackDown* taping took place that night. Fans attending the Charlotte Coliseum in North Carolina watched as Austin moved the crane arm forward to drop a cement girder onto the bus. Instead, the girder turned straight toward the glass cab Stone Cold sat in, stopping about six inches from hitting it before turning back the other way.

Triple H's account of the incident in the 2009 book *The Unauthorized History of DX* echoed Austin's recollection. The Game also noted that when the Rattlesnake regained control of the wildly swinging girder and hit the bus . . . nothing happened.

In fact, it took several long minutes in front of the Coliseum crowd before the girder set off the explosives attached around the bus.

Thankfully, because the show was shot on a Tuesday, the segment was heavily re-edited in postproduction. When *SmackDown* aired on TV Friday night, footage of the out-of-control girder was removed, as were the long delays before the girder finally made the bus explode.

2:88

WICK-IPEDIA

In the 2013 action thriller *The Package*, Steve Austin is a mob courier forced to fend off assassins so he can deliver a mysterious package to a crime lord known as "The German" (played by Austin's *The Expendables* co-star Dolph Lundgren). The name of Austin's mob enforcer character is Tommy Wick. *The Package* is written by Derek Kolstad, who the following year made a name for himself as the creator of the monstrously successful *John Wick* franchise.

2:89

TOO MUCH OF A GOOD THING

Though it didn't appear on the live broadcast of *Raw* March 22, 1999, Stone Cold Steve Austin thought he'd enjoy a quick taste of the beer he shot from a high-powered nozzle that floored The Rock, Mr. McMahon, and Shane McMahon. With his enemies laid out in the ring, Austin, figuring he'd sneak in a quick sip, turned the nozzle onto himself. He hadn't quite expected the force of the beer to come out quite so strong, however, and he momentarily knocked himself backward when the beer hit his face.

The Rattlesnake joked on the WWE home video *Hell Yeah: Stone Cold's Saga Continues* that the force from the hose was so strong that if he still had his tonsils, they would have been knocked down his throat.

2:90

TWO CLOSE

Only two years into his career, Steve Austin almost became a two-championship titleholder at a WCW The Great American Bash Tour event on August 25, 1991. "Stunning" Steve was already WCW World Television Champion when he defeated "The Z-Man," Tom Zenk and Barry Windham to advance to the finals of a WCW United States Heavyweight Title Tournament inside Atlanta's Omni Coliseum. He lost in the finals to Sting, who captured his first WCW U.S. Heavyweight Title that night.

Michael Cole: Earlier tonight, some controversial remarks [came] from Triple H concerning the Royal Rumble Match this Sunday, and we're just hoping to get your comments on what Triple H had to say . . .

[*Austin proceeds to tell Cole and the WWE Universe how he spent the night before in a Dallas bar, where he wore out a mechanical bull, threw patrons out of the bar, and answered the bartender's similar questions about Triple H.*]

Stone Cold: The one thing he'll never do is throw Stone Cold Steve Austin over the top rope. That just won't happen!

[*Crowd cheers.*]

I looked at that bartender and I said, "As a matter of fact, I'm workin' on my strategy right now."

Crowd: *What?*

Stone Cold: That's what *he* said. He said, "What?"

Crowd: *What?*

Stone Cold: I said, "I'm workin' on my strategy right now."

Crowd: *What?*

Stone Cold: I looked down at my waist and I said, "Do you see that?"

Crowd: *What?*

Stone Cold: He said, "What?"

Crowd: *What?*

Stone Cold: I said, "Do you see that?"

Crowd: *What?*

Stone Cold: That's what *he* said. He said, "What?"

Crowd: *What?*

Stone Cold: I said, "That's a beer belly."

Crowd: *What?*

Stone Cold: "A beer belly."

Crowd: *What?*

Stone Cold: "A beer belly!"

Crowd: *What?*

Stone Cold: "By lowerin' my center of gravity, it makes it hard for a man to throw me over the top rope."

Crowd: *What?*

Stone Cold: "That's Stone Cold Steve Austin's strategy. You understand what I'm talkin' about?" [*Crowd cheers.*] So, I looked at that bartender, and I said, "I ain't gonna mess with your mechanical bull no more. You can let everybody back in, 'cause I'm gonna drink every single beer you got to work on this beer belly." He said, "What?"

Crowd: *What?*

Stone Cold: "Beer belly!'"

Crowd: *What?*

Stone Cold: "Beer belly!"

Stone Cold and Crowd: *What?*

Stone Cold: "And while I'm workin' on this beer belly."

Crowd: *What?*

Stone Cold: "When I drink all your beer."

Crowd: *What?*

Stone Cold: "I'm goin' down to What-What-What-What-What-What-Whataburger."

Crowd: *What?*

Stone Cold: "And I'm gonna get a Whataburger with cheese." [*Crowd cheers.*] "A Whataburger *without* cheese."

Crowd: *What?*

Stone Cold: "A Whataburger with *double* cheese."

Crowd: *What?*

Stone Cold: "And French fries."

Crowd: *What?*

Stone Cold: "Some more French fries! And one of them fresh-catch fish sandwiches!"

Crowd: *What?*

Stone Cold: "Another Whataburger with double cheese!"

Crowd: *What?*

Stone Cold: "And I'm gonna roll in that Royal Rumble one pissed-off son of a bitch," because Triple H, you said you kicked my ass once?

Crowd: *What?*

Stone Cold: You said you kicked my ass once?

Crowd: *What?*

Stone Cold: So, you think you can do it again?

Crowd: *What?*

Stone Cold: That's what I said. I said, "What? *Eh-Ehh!*" And if you got a problem with that, I can say that to your face.

Crowd: *What?*

Stone Cold: I can say that to your side.

Crowd: *What?*

Stone Cold: I can say that to your back.

Crowd: *What?*

Stone Cold: I can say that to your *other* side.

Crowd: *What?*

Stone Cold: Or I can say that right to your face.

Crowd: *What?*

Stone Cold: Because the bottom line is Stone Cold Steve Austin is goin' to the *Royal Rumble* to win, to go to *WrestleMania*. And that's the bottom line — *What?* — 'cause Stone Cold said so!

Stone Cold lays out an interesting strategy heading into the 2002 Royal Rumble Match (*Raw*, January 14, 2002)

MARATHON RUMBLER

Because Stone Cold just doesn't have enough unbelievable Royal Rumble Match statistics, here's another: Of his six Royal Rumble Match appearances, Steve Austin had the longest in-ring time on three occasions — the only WWE Superstar at this point to have three.

In 1997, The Texas Rattlesnake lasted 45 minutes, 7 seconds to win the contest. As the No. 1 entrant in 1999, Austin achieved his longest Rumble match time at 56 minutes and 38 seconds, a time he shared with the bout's winner, No. 2 entrant Mr. McMahon. In his final Royal Rumble Match appearance in 2002, Austin endured in the ring for 26 minutes, 46 seconds. Amazingly, the three-time Royal Rumble Match winner was victorious only once in these three efforts.

In 2001, Stone Cold also set a record for winning the Royal Rumble Match in the shortest amount of time, clocking in at 9 minutes and 43 seconds. That record has since been surpassed several times, starting with Brock Lesnar in 2003 (8 minutes, 53 seconds).

STONE COLD VS. SANTA

On the December 22, 1997, edition of *Raw*, Stone Cold Steve Austin delivered season's beatings on the one and only Santa

Claus. Then again, it wasn't really Jolly Ol' St. Nick, or at least one *hopes* it wasn't, based on his in-ring behavior prior to Austin's arrival. This Santa griped that the beautiful Sable had no-showed him, then ordered a young boy out of the ring for calling him out as a crap Kringle. Stone Cold wasted no time in heading to the ring and giving Santa a little Christmas gift of his own: A Stunner and two birds that weren't turtle doves.

The young boy, by the way, was Jeremiah Fatu, the son of Rikishi and brother of Jimmy & Jey Uso.

2:94

AUSTIN-FOLEY III? NOT SO FAST

At one point, the plan was for Steve Austin and Mick Foley to follow up their hellacious Falls Count Anywhere Match at 1998's *Over the Edge* inside Hell in a Cell at *King of the Ring*. However, it was decided that, after two consecutive pay-per-views pitting Austin and Foley against each other, a change was needed. One could possibly debate that decision until *King of the Ring* — Stone Cold lost his championship in a vicious First Blood Match to Kane, while Foley, as Mankind, battled Undertaker inside what many to this day consider to be the seminal Hell in a Cell contest.

MAN BITES RATTLESNAKE

On the September 2, 2019, episode of *Straight Up Steve Austin*, "The Man" Becky Lynch added to her historic accolades by becoming the first woman to drop Stone Cold Steve Austin with his own finisher. While sharing a Steve Austin Broken Skull IPA with The Texas Rattlesnake, Lynch kicked Austin in the gut and hit the Stunner. She then told the prone Rattlesnake, "That's what happens when The Man comes around."

MAKING THE MOST OUT OF 'MANIA

Stone Cold Steve Austin amassed an extremely respectable 5–2 record at The Showcase of the Immortals, though he never entered any of his seven *WrestleMania* matches as WWE Champion. Austin went in as the challenger for three WWE Title clashes at The Show of Shows, and he left with the championship all three times. That ties him with Hulk Hogan and John Cena. Cena won his third WWE Championship (fourth World Title overall) on The Grandest Stage of Them All after defeating the Superstar Austin had beaten twice for the title, The Rock, at *WrestleMania 29*.

"For the last few weeks, I come out here and I sit here and listen to you spin your little nursery rhymes about 'Jabroni Avenue' or 'Know Your Role Boulevard.' Jesus Christ, son, you better get your ass serious because Stone Cold Steve Austin is gonna take his ass to Philadelphia, check right into the SmackDown Hotel, roll right into room 316 and *burn that son of a bitch to the ground*!"

Stone Cold's sobering words to WWE Champion The Rock before he soaks The Great One, Mr. McMahon, and Shane McMahon in hundreds of gallons of beer (*Raw*, March 22, 1999)

OH, HALL, YEAH!

Leave it to Stone Cold to raise some hell during introductions to the WWE Hall of Fame's Class of 2009 at the *25th Anniversary of WrestleMania*. After all inductees appeared on the stage inside Houston's Reliant Stadium, Steve Austin walked to the back for a minute. When he reappeared, he had gotten rid of the suit he'd worn and rode out in his Polaris 700cc, four-wheel "Redneck Special." The Texas Rattlesnake drove his "Austin 3:16"-themed ATV down the ramp and around the ring several times, then toasted the 72,000-plus WWE Universe members in attendance with some Steveweisers. It was definitely one of the hall's livelier introduction ceremonies at the annual Showcase of the Immortals.

NO "STEPS" IN HIS HOUSE

While working in World Championship Wrestling, Steve Austin met his biological father, James Anderson, at a live event. Since he was a baby when Anderson left the family, Austin described in his 2003 autobiography that the experience "was like talking to a stranger." Though he had no real feelings for Anderson, he bore no bitterness toward him, either. Austin has always maintained that despite not being biologically related, Ken Williams is the only father he has ever had.

3:00

"Hell, I was havin' fun with him the whole night. I wasn't gonna shoot him or cut him or anything like that . . . You know, as smart as Vince is, to finally put one over on him, means you done somethin'. The little flag comes out on the gun, 'Bang,' and he pissed his pants. I got a kick out of it myself."

The Bionic Redneck revels in the evening's *Raw* torment of "shooting" Mr. McMahon with a toy pistol with a scroll that says "Bang 3:16" (from *Hell Yeah: Stone Cold's Saga Continues*)

END OF AN ERA TIMES TWO

Fully Loaded's First Blood Match between Stone Cold Steve Austin and Undertaker (July 25, 1999) was also the first billed "End of an Era" contest in WWE. The second "End of an Era" clash came 13 years later at *WrestleMania XXVIII* (April 1, 2012), in a Hell in a Cell Match between Triple H and Undertaker.

WHO WANTS A BROKEN SKULL RANCH MARGARITA?

Beer may be Steve Austin's go-to beverage — particularly his Broken Skull IPA — but damn, he makes a fine margarita. It's a skill he mastered while living in south Texas, where a good margarita was hard for him to come by. The concoction Austin developed, the Broken Skull Ranch Margarita, may floor you faster than a Stone Cold Stunner.

Here are the ingredients, presented in "What?" style:

- Get a 3 oz. shot glass, a shaker, and a lowball glass.

What?

- Pour 3 oz. of Patrón Silver tequila into the shaker.

What?

- Pour in 1 to 1.5 oz. of triple sec.

What?

- Add 1 to 1.25 oz. of legit lime juice — that means squeeze some actual limes.

What?

- See some agave juice? Add a pinch.

What?

- Shake (don't stir) and pour the shaker's contents into your lowball glass.

What?

- Make sure that glass has fresh ice in it and salt on the rim.

What?

- Float an ounce of Grand Marnier on top of your margarita.

What?

- Add a lime to the glass rim.

What?

Bottom line: Drink up!

3:03

ELIMINATION DOMINATION

Of his six Royal Rumble Match appearances, Stone Cold Steve Austin notched the most Superstar eliminations on four occasions, a feat that remains unmatched to this day. In winning the

30-Superstar, over-the-top-rope classic in 1997, the Rattlesnake eliminated 10 Superstars, a Rumble record that lasted four years. Austin followed that up the following year with a second consecutive Rumble win and seven eliminations (a total he'd repeat in his final Royal Rumble Match in 2002). In 1999, The Texas Rattlesnake led all Superstars in eliminations for a third straight year by tossing eight more entrants to the outside floor.

Austin scored 36 eliminations in total throughout his Rumble career, a figure that led the pack until Shawn Michaels surpassed it in 2010. His total currently puts him in fourth place all-time, behind Kane, HBK, and Undertaker, respectively.

3:04

GO DIRECTLY TO JAIL

From 1997 until 2002, Stone Cold Steve Austin was "arrested" on WWE programming on eight separate occasions. For some, that might be a disturbing trend. For The Texas Rattlesnake, it came with the territory of raisin' hell against adversaries like Mr. McMahon, The Rock, and Triple H. Austin's most famous on-screen arrest arguably remains his first, following the inaugural Stone Cold Stunner he gave Vince McMahon on *Raw* September 22, 1997.

STEVE AUSTIN ... UNMARKETABLE?

"**S**tunning" Steve Austin was no doubt stunned himself when then-WCW president Eric Bischoff once suggested that he head to ECW or New Japan Pro-Wrestling, or perhaps even find something else to do for a living. According to Austin in multiple interviews and in his book *The Stone Cold Truth*, Bischoff explained that the WCW star's look was not something he could really market. Bischoff disputed the claim on his *83 Weeks* podcast in March 2020.

IT'S STONE COLD'S RING

For years, Steve Austin has displayed his fascination with skulls in the form of a skull ring on his right hand. He got his band — a Brotherhood of the Skull ring — at Silverlust Fine Jewelry, based out of Houston. The jeweler began making the ring after a musician had requested they make one similar to the ring rock icon Keith Richards wore on the October 6, 1988, cover of *Rolling Stone* magazine. Silverlust added a distinct look to their ring by smoothing and shaving down the sides of the skull.

Stone Cold: You got somethin' to say to me? You wanna talk about the Royal Rumble?

Michael Cole: Why, yeah, I'd love to ask you about –

Stone Cold: What?

Michael Cole: I'd love to ask you about —

Stone Cold: What? You gonna ask Stone Cold who's gonna win the Royal Rumble?

Crowd: *What?*

Stone Cold: It's Stone Cold!

Crowd: *What?*

Stone Cold: I said Stone Cold!

Crowd: *What?*

Stone Cold: Stone Cold!

Crowd: *What?*

Stone Cold: What part of "Stone Cold" do you not understand?

Crowd: *What?*

Stone Cold: Twenty-nine pieces of trash!

Crowd: *What?*

Stone Cold: Over the top rope!

Crowd: *What?*

Stone Cold: That includes Triple H!

Crowd: *What?*

Stone Cold: Kurt Angle!

Crowd: *What?*

Stone Cold: The Undertaker!

Crowd: *What?*

Stone Cold: The bottom line!

Crowd: *What?*

Stone Cold: The bottom line!

Crowd: *What?*

Stone Cold: The bottom line is Stone Cold Steve Austin is gonna win the Royal Rumble and go to *WrestleMania*, and that's the bottom line — *What?* — 'cause Stone Cold said so!

Stone Cold doesn't mince words for Michael Cole
or Atlanta's Philips Arena before the Royal Rumble
Match (*Royal Rumble*, January 20, 2002)

TIME TO LAYETH THE FIRST *SMACKDOWN*

Now *this* is a main event worthy of the pilot episode of *Smack-Down*: Stone Cold Steve Austin & The Rock — bitter enemies fighting over Austin's WWE Title just days before at *Backlash* — teaming up against Undertaker & Triple H, united under The Phenom and Shane McMahon's newly forged Corporate Ministry. The Tag Team Match ended in a No Contest, but seeing WWE's "Core Four" in *SmackDown*'s inaugural main event on April 29, 1999, marked a huge victory for WWE and its return to network television. Plus, Austin got to see Mr. McMahon take a downright savage chair blast before he Stunnered Undertaker and Shane-O-Mac, so he certainly felt like a winner that night.

YOU'RE IN GOOD HANDS WITH STONE COLD

Back when he was Steve Williams, Steve Austin entered Wharton County Junior College on a full scholarship as a business major. He thought he'd follow in his father's footsteps and one day take over his insurance business. Turns out he was better at forcibly convincing sports entertainers to take out insurance claims on themselves.

A DOG- AND CAT-LOVING RATTLESNAKE

Stone Cold may be merciless to his opponents within the confines of a 20' x 20' ring, but Steve Austin has a soft spot for dogs. Austin has had multiple canine companions over the years, and his current social channels are often littered with pictures and videos of himself with his Labrador retrievers, Cali, Moolah, and Brownie. That stated, he also has a fondness for felines, including Pancho and Lefty, the pair that currently live with him and his wife.

Interestingly enough, there's a renowned dog trainer in Australia named Steve Austin. We're fairly certain that he doesn't have a championship pedigree that's comparable to The Texas Rattlesnake's.

MAIN EVENT STYLISHNESS

In his USWA and WCW days, Steve Austin had established himself as a proficient in-ring technician. Following his devastating injury at *SummerSlam 1997*, though, for Stone Cold to endure in WWE, he needed to drastically alter his in-ring style. Austin changed his finessed wrestling technique to more of a broader, brawling style — one that allowed him to work around his injury, take the fight outside the ring more, and use whatever means were at his disposal to give him the edge in a match. This change soon became recognized in sports entertainment as the "main-event style" and was adapted by many WWE Superstars in the late '90s and early 2000s. The style would eventually become less utilized after WWE's "Ruthless Aggression" era of Superstars became more prominent.